Praise for *Digital Communion*

"We've achieved enough distance from McLuhan to revisit him afresh. In this engaging book, Nick Ripatrazone deftly shows how McLuhan's prescience means he can still show us our future. As we emerge from a global pandemic, during which we have been digitally baptized in unexpected ways, McLuhan's insights about incarnate faith in a virtual world are more timely than ever. Ripatrazone, who combines sparkling prose with theological insight, is an ideal guide."

—James K. A. Smith, professor of philosophy,
Calvin University; editor in chief, *Image* journal; author
of *How (Not) to Be Secular* and *You Are What You Love*

"While McLuhan is widely regarded as a prophet of our digital age, few writers have taken on the religious foundation of his vision as seriously and compellingly as Nick Ripatrazone does in this remarkable book. *Digital Communion* is a masterpiece of biographical criticism, one that uncovers the Catholic roots of ideas that are now inscribed in our digital ecosystem and illuminates how the virtual might reimagine the sacred. It utterly transformed how I think about McLuhan and the spiritual possibilities that still inflect contemporary technologies."

—Meghan O'Gieblyn, author of *God, Human,
Animal, Machine* and *Interior States*

"Nick Ripatrazone's *Digital Communion* is a joy to read. Meticulously researched, the book uncovers an often-sidelined aspect of Marshall McLuhan's media theories—their spiritual foundations—by imaginatively weaving biography, historical analyses, and critical readings of McLuhan's writings, as well as of other writings crucial to his thinking."

—Diletta De Cristofaro, Research Fellow in
the Humanities, Northumbria University, UK;
author of *The Contemporary Post-Apocalyptic Novel*

DIGITAL COMMUNION

DIGITAL COMMUNION

MARSHALL MCLUHAN'S
SPIRITUAL VISION FOR A VIRTUAL AGE

NICK RIPATRAZONE

FORTRESS PRESS
MINNEAPOLIS

DIGITAL COMMUNION
Marshall McLuhan's Spiritual Vision for a Virtual Age

Cover image: Joshua Eckstein / Unsplash
Cover design: LUCAS Art & Design, Jenison, MI

Print ISBN: 978-1-5064-7114-3
eBook ISBN: 978-1-5064-7115-0

For Amelia, Olivia, and Jennifer

Contents

Preface

Broadcast Religion

Calls flooded the switchboard at Yankee Stadium in late September 1965. People wanted tickets for the hottest show in town—and operators had to turn away scores of unhappy fans. Such late-season demand wouldn't be surprising, except that the New York Yankees were having one of their worst seasons in decades. They'd recently lost their final home game of the season against the Chicago White Sox, played in front of a paltry crowd of 10,419 fans.

Operators had to refer excited callers to the chancery of the archdiocese of New York,[1] because callers were pining for tickets to see Pope Paul VI, who was planning a momentous, one-day trip to New York City. The pope would soon pack 90,000 into Yankee Stadium to celebrate a Mass that would be broadcast worldwide—and foretell the electronic future of religion.

"People don't come to us now," English cardinal John Heenan had recently lamented. "We must go to them."[2] Pope Paul VI took that worry to heart. "Yes," he said, "the Pope is becoming a missionary, which means a witness, a shepherd, an apostle on the move."[3] This apostle moved more than four thousand miles on an Alitalia DC-8, landing at the airport named for the first Catholic president, the late John F. Kennedy.

The trip was unprecedented. Paul VI was the first pontiff to visit America. The city's police commissioner assigned eighteen thousand police officers to the visit, stationing them along the pope's route and at events. He urged New Yorkers to "stay off the streets" and instead "watch the event on television."[4] In addition to the Mass at Yankee Stadium, the pope was scheduled to meet with President Lyndon B. Johnson, give a speech at the United Nations, journey to Saint Patrick's Cathedral, and conclude with a visit to Michelangelo's *Pietà* displayed at the New York World's Fair.

Wooden barricades lined sidewalks along the papal motorcade route. Windows of stores near Saint Patrick's Cathedral were boarded up. Subways planned to run on frantic rush-hour schedules during his visit. Sisters at Cathedral High School in the Bronx were told the night before that ninety thousand copies of the pope's homily were needed. The high school didn't have enough paper, so the sisters sent messengers around the city to other schools and churches and finally finished their work at two in the morning—with enough time for a nap before morning

Mass.[5] The pope's fourteen-hour visit, like its preparations, would be a whirlwind. In authentic New York City fashion, one bartender was quoted as having a simple concern: "When will he get a chance to eat?"[6]

Everyone, it seemed, was ready for the pope—except the city's largest newspaper, the *New York Times*. The publication was on strike, along with most of the city's other papers. Editors and managers at the *Times* thought "the Newspaper Guild, particularly its many Catholic members, would find a way of settling the strike in time to cover one of the most challenging stories in the city's history."[7]

They didn't, but A. M. Rosenthal, the paper's metropolitan editor, got an unusual reprieve. Bantam Books recruited the striking staff to work on contract to produce an "instant book" about the pope's visit.[8] It was a frantic scene: They rented chairs and tables from a catering company and borrowed the bookkeeping department's typewriters.[9] Powered by urns of coffee, trays of sandwiches, and whiskey, they worked all through the day and night of the pope's visit, and the manuscript and photos were flown to Chicago the following morning. *The Pope's Journey to the United States* "had taken sixty-six and a half hours to produce" and was listed in the Guinness Book of World Records as "Fastest Publication."[10]

By that time, Pope Paul VI was back at the Vatican. Old news, however fast, is still old. The book was a valiant, impressive effort—but the fact remained that the city's traditional mode of journalism missed an iconic event. The answer to the darkness of local print media was a different medium: television.

All three major networks—NBC, ABC, and CBS—carried continuous television coverage of the pope's visit without commercial interruption.[11] Coverage started in the morning and continued well into the evening. Networks pooled their resources, devoting eighty-five cameras to the visit, the most collected for reporting a single story.[12] The broadcast results were staggering: between one hundred and two hundred million people in the United States, Canada, and Mexico watched some of the events, and two hundred million people in Great Britain and Western Europe viewed them by satellite.[13] The *Philadelphia Inquirer* took note of this grand occasion: "The significance of [Pope Paul VI's] journey is calculable not only in the momentous message of peace he delivered at the United Nations but in the tremendous outpouring of millions of persons of every race and creed in New York and the hundreds of millions of every nationality who followed proceedings throughout the day by television or radio around the earth. Never before in the span of time has the attention of so many focused simultaneously in a single direction and on a common goal: peace for mankind."[14]

Pope Paul VI was aware of the ecumenical, international electronic moment. He quoted Romans 1:8 during his homily at Yankee Stadium: "Your faith is proclaimed all over the world." Although liturgical reforms called for most of the service to be spoken in the local vernacular, Paul chose Latin "to emphasize the universality of the mass."[15] Police officers stationed around the track "alternated their Latin responses with objurgations to keep the entrance clear" for processions.[16] The old tongue blended with the new tongue—with many tongues, as the Apostle's

Creed was recited in English, French, Spanish, Russian, and Chinese. The stadium's audience was silent in reverence for much of the Mass; only "a rhythmic beat could be heard over the public-address system"—likely the sound of the pope's heart beating through the microphone on his chest.[17]

For a few hours, electronic communion thrived worldwide. Less than a decade later, Pope Paul VI appointed a Canadian professor of literature—Marshall McLuhan—to the Pontifical Council for Social Communications. Tall, eclectic, and able to pontificate on most any subject, the Cambridge-educated scholar had shifted from an academic focus on poetry to examinations of pop culture. It seemed like the perfect fit: the television pope would be advised by the electric oracle, the one person who seemed to truly understand the effects of the new electronic media.

McLuhan, a Catholic convert, seemed excited at the prospect of advising a church grappling with the results of electronic modernity. But while he would receive notices of meetings in Rome and tried to engage in dialogue with other committee members, it was to no avail. The silence was "a source of great disappointment."[18] The darling of secular print and television media was largely ignored by his own church while that church was grappling with how to remain essential in a rapidly changing world. McLuhan was truly the one for the job: He was erudite, confident, playful, and pious. He was an observer and predictor of trends. In short, he paid attention to the constantly evolving world, and he knew that intellectual risks, and the occasional failure, were necessary to understand that world. It was a lost opportunity.

* * *

"What if he's right?"

Tom Wolfe wondered if Marshall McLuhan—sitting "in a little office on the edge of the University of Toronto that looks like the receiving bin of a second-hand book store, grading papers, *grading papers*, for days on end"— was right.[19] Wolfe's buoyant prose and expansive eye were the perfect journalistic match for an eccentric character like McLuhan, who was having a cultural moment. A month after Pope Paul VI rode the airwaves to the ends of the earth, Wolfe was contemplating if McLuhan was the "oracle of the modern times."[20]

He had good reason to wonder. Earlier that year, during an appearance on the CBC show *Take 30*, McLuhan lamented that modern people have to rush in traffic to work—that we are perpetually stuck in a pattern of moving: "Documents, contracts, data. All of these materials actually could be just as available on closed-circuit at home."[21] McLuhan had recently published *Understanding Media*, in which he argued that television returned us to our tribal origins—emotional and experiential distance was extinguished by this medium. People were once again together. McLuhan thought the medium was more significant than its mere content; he implored us to examine the implicit and explicit *effects* of media. In the same way that print had transformed the manuscript—and therefore transformed knowledge and culture—he believed that television would change us. And McLuhan warned that television would be followed by something even more transfiguring.

Wolfe's question was pondered by other journalists, broadcasters, and executives who made McLuhan a media star, a public intellectual of the most public variety. In the 1960s and '70s, McLuhan was everywhere. He was the subject of feature articles in *Esquire, Vogue, Mademoiselle, Time, Fortune, Life, Newsweek,* the *New Yorker,* the *Nation, Harper's,* the *Los Angeles Times, Maclean's, Family Circle, Look,* the *Saturday Review, Playboy,* the *National Review,* and the *New York Times*—which had twenty-seven articles about him in 1967 alone.[22]

NBC featured an hour-long documentary on McLuhan, helmed by two Oscar-winning directors. He appeared on *The Today Show* and *The Tomorrow Show,* and on *The David Frost Show* alongside actor Peter Fonda. He made regular appearances on CBC programs and debated contemporary novelist Norman Mailer several times. Goldie Hawn's occasional line on the comedy show *Laugh-In* was "Whatcha doin', Marshall McLuhan?"—a line John Lennon quipped when he and Yoko Ono sat for an interview with the media theorist. McLuhan even made an infamous cameo as himself in the film *Annie Hall.* In short, McLuhan was everywhere someone *could* be—far more places than anyone expected an intellectual might be.

The one place he wasn't was the University of British Columbia in February 1965, during its Festival of the Contemporary Arts dedicated to him. "The Medium Is the Message," organized by architecture professors at the university, was built at the campus armory. Plastic sheets, suspended from the ceiling, draped "to form a maze that people wandered through in no particular sequence."[23] Organizers aimed slide projectors "at the ceiling, at the plastic curtains, onto the floor, or splattering the crowd itself with abstract projected images."[24] Loudspeakers blared odd sounds. A movie depicting the armory itself—albeit empty—streamed to confused looks. Dancers gyrated between visitors. Someone, somewhere, hammered a piece of wood.

It was sensory overload, a sensory reset. It was done in the name of McLuhan, but he was nowhere to be found. This wasn't his scene. This was the McLuhan paradox: he wasn't of the world of happenings and psychedelics, and yet, according to Timothy Leary, it was McLuhan himself who created the slogan "Turn on, tune in, drop out."

McLuhan was, to borrow the words of Thomas Merton, in the world and not of it.

* * *

The final page of the cover story of *Time* magazine's infamous 1966 "Is God Dead?" issue is a single column—with two-thirds of the page devoted to an advertisement for the 5010 Computyper electronic billing and accounting machine by Friden. One major selling point is the machine's ability to save time, especially with complex invoices for things like lumber, which typically require measurement changes. "Conversions are instantaneous and accurate," advertisements promised.[25]

McLuhan would have appreciated that type of juxtaposition: a cosmic wink, perhaps. In the same way, McLuhan's method of writing and thinking was the mosaic, a constellation of quotations, meditations, questions—probes. The mosaic is a precursor to hypertext; words linked to more words, phrases, references, routes. A code of thinking.

At the heyday of his fame, McLuhan was a source of envy, confusion, admiration, and criticism. Critics were uncomfortable with calling McLuhan a "prophet," thinking he was a shamanistic visionary whose apparent ability to predict the future created cultic devotion or that he was a huckster whose abstract visions were only a step above Nostradamus. Some criticisms pilloried his prose style; others aimed for his ego. Most criticisms would be proven wrong as time passed and McLuhan's wild predictions became mundane reality.

More than anything else, McLuhan was a Catholic. The man who understood the new world better than most was fueled by an old belief. He was guarded about the spiritual elements of his media theories, but McLuhan's entire project was a complex investigation into a second coming—an electronic communion.

As contemporary theologians pondered if God was dead, McLuhan considered how God had become transformed. In perhaps his most famous book, the text-and-art amalgam *The Medium Is the Massage*, McLuhan juxtaposed his statement that "the Newtonian God—the God who made a clock-like universe, wound it, and withdrew—died a long time ago" below a photograph depicting six women making a quilt, with the saying "Keep in circulation the rumor that God is alive."[26] It was the slogan for a February 1966 television ad campaign from the National Council of Churches who said the commercials hoped to "stimulate the viewer to think about where he stands with God."[27]

McLuhan would appreciate such a campaign, but he had his own theory. "Suddenly really got the 'God is dead' message," he wrote in his journal. "They mean that the Incarnation was His death because He became visible. Now in the non-visual time, the visual alienates them."[28]

McLuhan thought the print world was visual; the electric world—especially television—was a medium of touch. It enveloped us. For McLuhan, God was everywhere, including in the electric light.

What if McLuhan was right? *Digital Communion* will reveal that he was.

Introduction

A Conversion

"I have never been an optimist or a pessimist. I'm an apocalyptic only," Marshall McLuhan said during a 1977 interview.[1] "Apocalypse is not gloom," he added. "It's salvation."[2] If we embrace the religious import of McLuhan as electronic *prophet*, then his cataclysmic tone feels not only appropriate but necessary. Prophets see, they beckon, they disrupt. For McLuhan, prophecy existed in a tradition that led to the end of all things through the parousia—a world made utterly, divinely new.

McLuhan, the pop culture sage of the electronic world, was a Catholic convert. The entertainment, media, and academic worlds of his heyday had good reason to miss the Christian foundations of his theories, for there is evidence that McLuhan, sly rhetorician that he was, made subtle his

1

overtly religious sense. Yet it is telling that some of his earliest and most vocal defenders and explicators were Jesuit priests—intellectuals who were equally comfortable wading through esoteric theology as they were moving among the secular masses.

In 1967, John M. Culkin, then a Jesuit based at Fordham University, wrote an essay for the *Saturday Review* that sought to make McLuhan's ideas understandable to a mainstream audience. "McLuhan's writings abound with aphorisms, insights, for-instances, and irrelevancies which float loosely around recurring themes," the priest wrote.[3] McLuhan, he noted, was an observer of current trends, not a creator of them; "he is merely trying to describe what's happening out there so that it can be dealt with intelligently." After all, when "someone warns you of an oncoming truck, it's frightfully impolite to accuse him of driving the thing."[4] McLuhan was bearing witness.

McLuhan's Christian belief and worldview are no mere biographical footnote; they offer him pliable metaphors for the intersection of the material and the spiritual, they engender him with the confidence and determination of a religious adherent, and they compel him to react to the rapidly changing electronic world around him. Any honest and thorough analysis of McLuhan's paradigm-changing views must not merely begin with these religious considerations but also examine how his belief sustained the development and dissemination of these theories. McLuhan's vocation was to understand how the environments created by media shape our perception of the world.

Born on July 21, 1911, McLuhan regularly attended Nassau Baptist Church, minutes away from his home in

Edmonton, Alberta, Canada.[5] Years later, McLuhan's son Eric would say that his father "was raised in a loose sort of Protestantism,"[6] where religious piety was less present than a strong sense of culture—young McLuhan read English poetry and practiced elocution with his mother, a talented speaker and actress.[7]

McLuhan likely drifted toward agnosticism at the University of Manitoba, where he enrolled in 1928.[8] He began as an engineering major but switched to English and kept a diary of quotations from his reading—a style that influenced the mosaic method of his books, where ideas and references from myriad sources would juxtapose and intertwine. While an undergraduate, he began reading Shakespeare and the Bible each night before bed, and by the time he turned nineteen, he wrote that he wanted to become a better person and wished to learn how to properly pray.[9] He graduated from Manitoba with his BA in 1933 and his MA the following year, receiving a scholarship for postgraduate study at Cambridge. It was quite the change for the boy raised in—according to his own framing—agrarian Canada, which offered him an outside view of the social and intellectual world.[10] He enjoyed his time at Cambridge and studied with esteemed scholars, including F. R. Leavis, I. A. Richards, and A. E. Housman. There he read Jacques Maritain, T. S. Eliot, Virginia Woolf, and two writers who remained essential for his entire life: Gerard Manley Hopkins and James Joyce (August 6, 1935: "Reading Joyce *very* slowly").[11]

Along with Hopkins and Joyce there was another Catholic influence: G. K. Chesterton. The prolific Catholic convert was a fixture of BBC radio, and by 1934,

McLuhan was ripe for such inspiration. In October of that year, McLuhan was already writing to his brother about Catholicism: "Now concerning your intention to read further concerning Catholic ideas respecting images and doctrine—you need go no further than the succinct and admirable little volume" by the British Jesuit Father Martin D'Arcy.[12] McLuhan wrote a letter to his family praising the poetry of T. S. Eliot—mentioning several times the poet's Anglo-Catholic identity—but lamented how there were not many critics who have the religious background and sense to truly understand him.[13] It was a strangely prescient observation that foretold the inability of secular and even religious commentators to understand McLuhan's own project.

His Catholic meandering became something more in a September 1935 letter to his mother. She had cautioned that his so-called religion-hunting in the direction of Catholicism might imperil his academic job search. McLuhan responded with a full-blown Catholic apologia, writing that the Catholic religion "is alone in blessing and employing all those merely human faculties which produce games and philosophy, and poetry and music and mirth and fellowship with a very fleshy basis."[14] McLuhan affirmed that Catholic culture created Chaucer, Don Quixote, Saint Francis, and Rabelais and praised their "various and rich-hearted humanity."[15]

"Had I not encountered Chesterton," he proclaimed, "I would have remained agnostic for many years at least."[16] McLuhan was especially drawn to the Catholic view of the bodily and communal elements of the incarnation and resurrection of Christ. For Catholics, God is with us in form

4

and spirit, demonstrated through the liturgy of Mass, the veneration of saints and relics, and the Eucharist. In contrast, McLuhan claimed that his mother's version of faith implies "that the map of the universe was not radically altered" by the incarnation and the resurrection.[17] He concluded, "Let me tell you that religion is not a nice comfortable thing that can be scouted by cultivated lectures. . . . It is veritably something which, if it could be presented in an image, would make your hair stand on end."[18] His letter should be read not as from a son merely disrespecting his mother but rather as from a seeker on the precipice of conversion teeming with curiosity and sincerity, feeling more than a little defensive.

Chesterton, who McLuhan once described sounding on BBC radio "like a wheezy old Colonel,"[19] had an indelible influence on him: "I know every word of him: he's responsible for bringing me into the church."[20] Chesterton's aptly titled humor-tinged jeremiad *What's Wrong with the World* was an especially strong influence on McLuhan, offering him a template for how Catholicism could be both a religion and a cultural worldview.[21] Even Chesterton's rhetorical flourishes, down to the levels of syntax and rhythm, influenced McLuhan's prose and speeches. Chesterton's lines like "The Christian ideal has not been tried and found wanting. It has been found difficult, and left untried" left lasting impressions on McLuhan.[22] One of McLuhan's earliest publications was an essay, "G. K. Chesterton: A Practical Mystic" in the *Dalhousie Review*. McLuhan lauded Chesterton's "mastery of epigram and sententious phrase,"[23] which delivered "mysteries"—"the daily miracles of sense and consciousness."[24] McLuhan's assessment of Chesterton is an apt description of himself: "It is plain that he is literally a radical, because he goes to the roots of things."[25]

Chesterton was not the only Catholic radical who formed McLuhan. In his spiritual letter to his mother, McLuhan quotes lines from Gerard Manley Hopkins: "But good grows wild and wide, / Has shades, is nowhere none."[26] McLuhan had recently bought a book of Hopkins poems with the last of some extra money that he had saved.[27] It was not his first encounter with the enigmatic British Jesuit. McLuhan had spent the summer of 1932 walking and biking through England while reading poetry. "'Pied Beauty,' the single poem of Hopkins in my copy, was quite startling," he recalled. "I assumed he was a Victorian eccentric who had been noted for one or two small poems such as this."[28]

McLuhan would go on to identify Hopkins's eccentricity as genius. "The *effects* of new media on our sensory lives are similar to the effects of new poetry," he proclaimed. "They change not our thoughts but the structure of our world."[29] From Gutenberg to the present, McLuhan was interested in moments of transformation, and Hopkins offered a poetic revolution, a prosody and aesthetic that were out of time and place. McLuhan would say that Hopkins must be read "aloud. He *insists* on it!"[30] Hopkins had become a Catholic himself while at Oxford, so McLuhan, a Christian turned agnostic turned Catholic seeker, had found not simply an example but a precedent.

One of McLuhan's earliest appearances in an American literary magazine was an essay on Hopkins for the *Kenyon Review* in 1944. He warns that Hopkins "is full of pitfalls for the unwary," including his Catholic faith, his language, and "his irrelevant theory of prosody."[31] McLuhan explains that while Catholics like the fact that Hopkins is universally respected as a poet, their affinity for him tends to be one of shared doctrine; they are often confused by his syntax and style. But McLuhan thinks the effort to parse the poetry has just rewards, for Hopkins can shift "his gaze from the order and perspectives of nature to the analogous but grander scenery of the moral and intellectual order."[32] Essentially, the small and ordinary were representations of the grand and sacred for Hopkins. Poetry's layers of meaning and varying registers of language—to use McLuhan's schema—make the art form an especially dynamic medium.

McLuhan's careful reading of "The Windhover"—a notoriously dense, wrought, and yet beautiful poem by Hopkins—reveals several things: McLuhan was methodical, creative, associative, open-minded, and exceedingly comfortable viewing literature and life through a religious lens. He posits that Hopkins was a poet of patterns: "A relatively small number of themes and images—such is the intensity of his perception—permits him an infinitely varied orchestration."[33] He was drawn to Hopkins's "bursts into colloquial phrase," as in "God's Grandeur," where "he suddenly brings the sinews of English into play by strong gestures and abrupt incongruities of imagery, such as any newspaper provides regularly and unintentionally."[34] In one sentence, McLuhan is able to praise Hopkins's prosody while also gently placing him in a tradition of media innovation.

In a 1959 speech to seminarians, McLuhan said that the artist's role "is not to stress himself or his own point of view but to let things sing and talk, to release the forms within them." Although he thought Hopkins's idiosyncratic terms such as instress, inscape, and sprung rhythm were "very quaint," their true collective spirit was sound: "The *thingness* of things must come through them at you and must not be reported or described." A Catholic vision of art is one grounded in the recognition that the artist is less creator than vessel for the Holy Spirit: "It restructures your outlook. It completely changes your attitudes, your wavelengths. So our attitudes, our sensibilities, are completely altered by new forms."[35]

Hopkins predated the electronic world that McLuhan would inhabit and explore, but the Jesuit's poetic sense transcended his medium. Of the poem "Pied Beauty," McLuhan says that "Hopkins offers new perception related to the new world that flowed across the old one"[36]—an enticing but complex observation that McLuhan renders elsewhere in a more contemporary way: "Hopkins anticipates the electronic age in perceiving nature itself as an art form."[37]

Hopkins brought together several elements that appealed to McLuhan: He was a convert, one who moved from what he perceived to be a passive Christianity to an active, spirited denomination and for whom the incarnation was a source of creativity and a beacon of truth. He was a poet who believed that words could channel the spirit and praise Christ. Most importantly, he was a man out of place, a radical outsider whose poems burst not only out of the page but out of language. "The endlessly astonishing fact about Hopkins," McLuhan wrote, "is the way in which he not only touches but escapes from his age."[38] As with Chesterton, McLuhan once again summarized himself when he described his influences.

Chesterton and Hopkins were enough of an intellectual combination to steel McLuhan's already existing drift toward Catholicism at Cambridge. He wrote to his brother in April 1936, "Had I come into contact with the Catholic Thing, the Faith, 5 years ago, I would have become a priest I believe."[39] The faith of his youth now seemed provincial and, perhaps worse for McLuhan, anti-intellectual: "I could never have respected a 'religion' that held reason and learning in contempt—witness the 'education' of our preachers. I have a taste for the intense cultivation of the Jesuit rather than the emotional orgies of an evangelist."[40]

Later that year, he wrote a letter to a priest friend of his mother, stating his interest in being received into the Church. During Christmas, when McLuhan came home to Canada, he met and spoke with the priest. In January 1937, McLuhan started going to Sunday Mass and met with Father Alvin Kutchera, who had just become pastor at the University of Wisconsin's Saint Paul's Catholic Center; McLuhan had a temporary teaching position at the university. Kutchera was known as an ecumenicist: "He helped drama instructors to understand Catholic ritual and symbolism. He opened the Catholic center to Protestants, zealously helped the development of Hebrew studies, and invited university officials to an annual dinner with the archbishop of Milwaukee."[41] McLuhan converted to Catholicism on March 24, 1937, with Father Kutchera receiving him into the Church.

Now when McLuhan spoke of Catholicism, he did so as a participant rather than as one with a mere intellectual curiosity. He lauded Mass and the reception of the Eucharist as "spiritual *acts*" in a 1939 letter to his wife. He found in Catholicism a certain equality of imperfection, that "one man is quite as great a sinner as the next."[42] As a convert, he was certainly inclined to draw comparisons and thought one distinction was that Catholics were drawn to God through love, not fear. He also placed himself within a lineage by writing that "most [Catholic] converts tend to be intellectuals."[43] Becoming a Catholic meant entering a spiritual drama, for "there is a great heightening of every moment of experience, since every moment is played against a supernatural backdrop."[44]

After his conversion, McLuhan had a spiritual worldview that felt sustained by an intellectual foundation and tradition. "I am conscious of a job to be done," McLuhan wrote in a letter dated 1946, "one that I can do, and, truly, I do not wish to take any step in it that is not consonant with the will of God." The recipient was Clement McNaspy, a Jesuit who McLuhan thought would understand his ambitious project. "My increasing awareness," he noted, "has been of the ease with which Catholics can penetrate and dominate secular concerns—thanks to an emotional and spiritual economy denied to the confused secular mind."[45] For McLuhan, faith resulted in clarity and confidence. Rather than an intellectual vise, belief charged the Catholic thinker.

Clarity and confidence were both necessary for a form of cultural battle. McLuhan wrote of the need to "confront the secular in its most confident manifestations, and, with its own terms and postulates, to shock it into awareness of its confusion, its illiteracy, and the terrifying drift of its logic." He thought there was "no need to mention Christianity" during the criticisms, for it "is enough that it be known that the operator is a Christian." McLuhan thought the battle "must be conducted on every front—every phase of the press, book-rackets, music, cinema, education, economics." The ultimate goal was to help "both Catholic and non-Catholic, to resist the swift obliteration of the person which is going on."[46] McLuhan did not desire to convert religiously but wished to convert perceptively. He publicly refrained from overt Christian references, "lest perception be diverted from structural processes by doctrinal sectarian passions."[47]

The Eucharist—that which McLuhan believed was both symbol and substance, metaphor and material—offered McLuhan a vessel for his media theories. "Analogy is not concept," he wrote. "It is community. It is resonance. It is inclusive. It is the cognitive process itself. That is the analogy of the divine Logos."[48] He was strident on this point: "I do not think of God as a concept, but as an immediate and ever-present fact—an occasion for continuous dialogue."[49] Additionally, "faith is not a matter of concepts; it's percepts, a matter of immediate reality."[50] Such a point of view would compel McLuhan to focus on the elements of life that were most replicated: the media that surround us and the God that permeates them all.

Jesus is the synthesis, for in him, "there is no distance or separation between the medium and the message: it is the one case where we can say that the medium and the message are fully one and the same."[51] In a similar vein, McLuhan stressed that "the church is a thing, and not a theory"—a community and belief so masterfully simple and true that "the poor and the children of the world can grasp it, whereas the wise and the learned have serious conceptual problems blocking their perceptual lives."[52] He cautioned that while theology "should ideally be a study of the *thingness*, the nature of God, since it is a form of contemplation," if God is imagined as "a theoretical or intellectual construct, it is purely a game."[53]

McLuhan felt comfortable critiquing the Church he joined. In 1977, McLuhan would claim that "the powerful forces imposed on us by electricity" have not "been considered at all by theologians and liturgists."[54] It is a grand claim in the tradition of McLuhan's broader proclamations, but it *felt* true to McLuhan and compelled him to consider the place of the Church in the electronic era. "The Church is watching its cultural infrastructure crumble beneath its feet," he lamented. He thought that the traditions of belief were endemic to our longings: to be human meant to have faith or be concerned with its absence. Yet he worried that "electric man has no bodily being. He is literally *dis*-carnate," which "is a tremendous menace to an incarnate Church, and its theologians haven't even deemed it worthwhile to examine the fact."[55]

Although McLuhan was concerned with those theologians and their perceived inability to engage the effects of the electronic world, he was far more interested in the liturgists. They had daily and weekly engagement with the masses; they were the celebrants and performers. McLuhan's concerns arose from relatively simultaneous, and ultimately connected, developments: the integration of microphones and speaker systems into churches and the shift to celebrating Mass in local vernacular. During the time of McLuhan's conversion in the late 1930s through the early 1960s, those religious services and experiences would have been in Latin. When McLuhan wrote that "language is the encoded form of the collective perceptions and wisdom of many people," and that "poetry and song are the major means by which a language purifies and invigorates itself," he implies that Latin Mass was language perfected through ritual.[56]

Latin was not the language of "most people, clergy and laity alike."[57] It was not the language of the dinner table, or the baseball game, or the secular academic. It was the language of ritual: the recognition that Mass was delivered in a solemn, antiqued tongue, with its antiquity resulting in a displacement of language. The words hung a bit longer in the air, and in the ear. Liturgical language was the "great organic and collective medium that assimilates and organizes the chaos of everyday experience."[58]

The electronic era of Latin Mass, McLuhan thought, was a disaster. Microphones make "an indistinct mumble intolerable" because "it accentuates and intensifies the sounds of Latin to the point where it loses all of its power."[59] The microphone on the altar, as it were, blared Latin so that it devolved from measured to meaningless. In this new acoustic space, there are no margins, and the center is everywhere; the speaker at the microphone "is everywhere simultaneously—a fact which 'obsolesces' the architecture of our existing churches."[60]

The switch to vernacular language was even worse; without the "oral dimension of popular idioms and rhythms" carried forth through tradition, the result was a "vacant lot and a spiritual desert."[61] The vernacular language mirrored everyday speech; concision and communication had overcome complexity and texture. The blessed mutter of the past—in its foreignness—"did not prevent people meditating and praying during the Mass, whereas the vernacular does prevent them."[62] Latin flowed like a background chant, but the vernacular, in its speaker-ready smoothness, took language from the tongue and put it in wires and cables. Gone was the solemnity, the otherness, of the service. Linguistically, Sunday sounded like any other day.

These changes especially mattered to McLuhan because the liturgy was his entrance to the faith.[63] It also redefined the priesthood. One "effect of the microphone is to turn the priest around to face the congregation, so that now he 'puts on' the congregation rather than putting on God."[64] Even the structure of the church—in fact, its efficacy as an architectural space built to praise God—was made superfluous, "since the loudspeakers in the church permit sounds to come from every direction, rendering the acoustics and the visual lay-out of the church meaningless."[65] He offered a useful and concise contrast: "The vernacular is strongly horizontal in its thrust and embrace, whereas Latin tended to the vertical and the specialist aspiration."[66]

On one hand, McLuhan thought the Word, in its purest sense, transcended its earthly mediums. While "any of the visible forms of the church could undergo total transformation and dissipation," those fragmentations "would have no relevance to the central reality and thingness of the revealed and divinely constituted Church."[67]

Yet McLuhan also entertained more ominous interpretations of the changes happening in the Church and the world. In a May 9, 1969, letter to the Catholic philosopher Jacques Maritain, McLuhan wrote that "electric information environments being utterly ethereal fosters the illusion of the world as spiritual substance." Rather than being a spiritual beacon, the electronic world was "a reasonable facsimile of the mystical body, a blatant manifestation of the Anti-Christ. After all, the Prince of this World is a very great electric engineer."[68] Several months later, in a letter to Father Robert J. Leuver, editor of *US Catholic* magazine, McLuhan again invoked the potential demonic nature of the electronic world, claiming that it is the devil's "master stroke to be not only environmental but invisible, for the environmental is invincibly persuasive when ignored."[69] He worried that a pretender could be mistaken for the one true Christ: "At such times it becomes crucial to hear properly and to tune yourself in to the right frequency."[70]

McLuhan was of two minds here. "Electric media," he observed, "have made mass assemblies possible."[71] McLuhan's puns are playful, but they aren't flippant. In fact, McLuhan viewed punning as a rhetorical tradition —a way to clothe content in language and appeal to our joy for rhythm and rhyme. "The Catholic church was founded on a pun, very naturally," he observed, referring to Matthew 16:18: "Thou art Peter, and upon this rock I will build my church."[72] Rather than being contradictory, McLuhan was authentically wrestling with the changing and frightening new world.

McLuhan knew the coming electronic world offered possibilities for the spreading of Christian faith—which, as a Catholic, he would see as necessary and good, while recognizing it could be the realm of tricksters, whose electronic blips were smoke and mirrors. "I have never endorsed the events I have described, nor have I ever condemned any of the things I analysed," McLuhan wrote in 1970. "I am interested in understanding processes. Such are the opaquities and obliquities of 'value' judgments that they have always stood in the way of human understanding. This applies as much to the revealed truth of the Catholic faith as [to] the artefacts of human ingenuity."[73]

McLuhan was certain that people of faith needed to be aware of these changes and confront them emotionally and spiritually rather than merely accepting them. "One of the peculiarities of the electric intercom is that it is the sender who is sent," he posited. "Thus electronic man tends toward the disembodied or discarnate condition of 'angel.' I suggest the incarnational Church has need to confront this new discarnate state of the laity under electronic conditions."[74] He was aware of the inherent paradoxes of the unfolding world. While he wondered if it could be possible that we might "participate in a common liturgy globally" and "all assist at the same Mass," he recognized that "if we want the entire world to be present, vernaculars, far from helping, pose a major obstacle."[75]

McLuhan was not a theologian. Yet he was a scholar of literature, a reader of texts. Years later, reflecting on his conversion, McLuhan explained that the Church "has a very basic requirement or set of terms, namely that you get down on your knees and ask for the truth." For several years before his conversion, he prayed to God that he be shown a sign, and finally that sign was "shown very suddenly." Before the journey of his conversion, he said, "I never had any need for religion, any personal or emotional crisis. I simply wanted to know what was true and I was told."[76] He said that he came into the Church on his knees, and that "is *the only* way in."[77]

It was inevitable that McLuhan's religious beliefs would be both foundation and structure for his media theories, because both God and the electronic world were omnipresent in their own ways. "When I study media *effects*," McLuhan explained, "I am really studying the subliminal life of a whole population, since they go to great pains to hide these effects from themselves."[78] Toronto's Archbishop Philip Pocock once asked McLuhan if the prologue to John's Gospel might represent Christ as the archetypal version of the medium as message, and McLuhan agreed.[79] McLuhan thought that reading the Bible needed to be a regular activity, so that it might "pass into your daily life," for only then "do you get the message, that is, the effect. Only in that moment do medium and message unite."[80]

Perhaps, then, the inevitable electronic world required a prophet—a person of faith—who might observe, document, describe, and gently offer suggestions. "The Church is the only institution capable of coping with this situation and is not very keen on it," McLuhan observed. "A new doctrine is needed that should have been promulgated one hundred years ago: at the instant of Incarnation, the structure of the universe was changed. All of creation was remade. There was a new physics, a new matter, a new world. The doctrine would enable modern man to take the Church much more seriously."[81] This new arrival, portending a second coming of sorts, would happen without our assent. "The new matrix is acoustic, simultaneous, electric—which in one way is very friendly to the Church.

That is, the togetherness of humanity is now total," he noted.[82] "As long as there is the means of communion, social and divine," McLuhan assured, "there is an indefinite number of forms in which it can be achieved."[83]

This simultaneous, complete communion could not be provincial. McLuhan believed that "it is especially the job of the Catholic humanist to build bridges between the arts and society today." This needed to be an active pursuit, not merely a mode of contemplation; otherwise, McLuhan explained, "our secular contemporaries" would master the world of electronic interaction and "use it for power over the minds of men."[84] A skeptical point of view, but a realistic one. What was needed was a person of faith who was willing to make grand pronouncements in the most public of venues, who was willing to be wrong and criticized. What was needed was a deft rhetorician with a love for language and a firm footing in intellectual and literary traditions. What was needed was a person who was serious in his self-effacements, who was in the world but never truly of the world. What was needed, essentially, was Marshall McLuhan.

1

The Word Made Wide

Johann Gutenberg "made all history simultaneous," Marshall McLuhan affirmed. "The transportable book brought the world of the dead into the space of the gentleman's library; the telegraph brought the entire world of the living to the workman's breakfast table."[1] *The Gutenberg Galaxy,* published in 1962, was his first expansive book. McLuhan articulated his goal on the first page: he "intended to trace the ways in which the *forms* of experience and of mental outlook and expression have been modified, first by the phonetic alphabet and then by printing."[2] He subtitled his book *The Making of Typographic Man* and gently warned his reader that his book "develops a mosaic or field approach to its problems." Linear historical inquiries, he thought, could not reveal "causal operations"—the complex routes toward present experiences. Rather, his chosen method was a "galaxy or constellation of events," which reveals "a mosaic of perpetually interacting forms that have undergone kaleidoscopic transformation—particularly in our own time."[3]

The printing press did not create the book, but the printing press transformed the book—and if the book being made was a sacred one, that transformation was more significant. In titling his book *The Gutenberg Galaxy*, McLuhan acknowledged the historical association of printing with the famous printer from Mainz—but he also wedded the transformative typographical world to religious texts. We might call this association clever or sly, and both modifiers would apply equally well to McLuhan's rhetorical sense.

Gutenberg's creations marked a turn in how words spread in a culture. For a theorist like McLuhan, who was more interested in method and environment than content, Gutenberg's Bible was an epoch-forming invention—and offered the key to understanding the coming electronic world.

Before Gutenberg, the *Catholicon*, a Latin dictionary finished by a Dominican priest in 1286, was widely read for nearly two centuries. Yet Gutenberg's 1460 edition was special. "With the help of the Most High at whose will the tongues of infants become eloquent and who often reveals to the lowly what he hides from the wise," reads the book's colophon, "this noble book *Catholicon* has been printed and accomplished without the help of reed, stylus or pen but by the wondrous agreement, proportion and harmony of punches and types."[4] The book's production seemed inspired; it sounded practically miraculous.

Agreement, proportion, and harmony: the song of that mechanical synthesis was being praised by its creator. Before

Gutenberg, Bibles and other books were the painstaking work of scribes, copying page after page in an exhausting process. Scriptoriums, as they were called, included not only scribes but also illuminators, rubricators, and binders whose wealthy customers expected high quality.[5] These wealthy families eventually wanted priests to celebrate Mass in their homes, and those priests wanted small texts that could be easily carried and handled.[6]

Mass required mass production. The Catholic Church was in need of texts: "missals, indulgences, Bibles, prayer books, song-sheets and Latin grammars on which the churches, monastaries, nunneries and schools depended." Dutiful scribes labored, but even the best among them could not produce more than "two high-quality, densely packed pages a week."[7] The supply could not meet the faithful's demand.

Mistakes were worse than the slow production. An errant translation would infect each subsequent hand-copied edition. While monasteries would certainly suffer from using poorly sourced reproductions, even more concerning for Church leaders was the potential for liturgical miscues. The Mass—that sacred celebration—demanded uniformity.[8]

Mechanical printing had existed in China, Japan, and Korea, but Eastern languages tended to be logographic and therefore too complex and expensive to reproduce.[9] Meanwhile, in 1451, Nicholas of Cusa, a German cardinal, argued for "the need for monastic libraries to possess a well-translated and edited Bible."[10] He wrote that "much of the Christian religion has degenerated to an appearance," and the best solution was consistency from parish to parish and region to region—a faith made uniform.[11]

At some point in the 1420s or 1430s, Nicholas of Cusa likely crossed paths with Gutenberg in Mainz, Germany. Gutenberg was chosen to create the new Bible, one that would be identical copy to copy, proofed and prepared and printed in a manner that could eclipse the most dedicated and skilled scribes. Gutenberg had punches, vellum, paper, and type. He had a structure: two columns. Perhaps he felt some divine—or ecclesiastically prosaic—calling, but either way, Gutenberg delivered 180 copies of his Bible. Enea Silvio Piccolomini, who would later become Pope Pius II, wrote to Cardinal Juan de Carvajal in March 1455 and noted that those copies of the Bible had quickly sold out.[12]

"Discourse was deemed man's noblest attribute," William Wordsworth wrote, "And written words the glory of his hand. / Then followed printing with enlarged command / For thought—dominion vast and absolute / For spreading truth and making love expand."[13] The word of God could now spread like never before, and spread it did—in various permutations. One of the first best-selling books was *The Imitation of Christ* by Thomas à Kempis.[14] As well, now mistakes in sacred texts could be fixed, rather than lingering in successive editions; as Elizabeth Eisenstein has noted, "Erasmus or Bellarmine could issue errata; Jerome or Alcuin could not."[15]

The word and world of God could only get bigger now, and the metaphorical implications of this shift cannot be understated. The Bible was destined for this growth. "There are also many other things that Jesus did," John writes in the final sentence of his Gospel, "but if these were to be described individually, I do not think the whole world would contain the books that would be written."[16] Saint Augustine, echoing John, wrote that the total commandments of God would constitute a "book of life," and "such a volume would be beyond fathoming in its size and length it should be understood as a certain divine power."[17] The idea of a book, then, exists as both vessel and wall; it is necessary to spread the word of God, and yet its physical traits are limiting. There will never be enough books to tell the stories of Jesus, not simply because there are not enough hands and scribes and rolls of paper, but because the life and love of Jesus resisted documentation in prosaic terms. The paradox of the religious text as a material toward spiritual enlightenment creates energy through its tension; the text needs believers in order to lift its words into transcendence.

In *The Lord of the Absurd*, his attempt to understand the nature of God in a chaotic world, Father Raymond J. Nogar considers how Thomas Aquinas argued that Jesus did not write down his teachings, for they were far too mysterious. The life of Jesus "had to be lived, to be acted out, as it were, in the presence of those who could personally understand with love." Perhaps complex Christian schemas were "highly limited systems which were destined to fall short in touching men's lives with Christ's mysterious love." Nogar wonders if the "meaning of the Cross" could ever possibly be encapsulated "in a doctrinal world-view, a picture of reality; or must that meaning of the Cross, of necessity, be lived out in a personal drama?"[18]

The tension between book and belief, material text and spiritual dogma, is an ancient tension—one endemic to a faith that seeks to sing the Word to all. The concept of the book abounds in the Bible. "Your eyes saw me unformed," the psalmist writes, "in your book all are written down; / my days were shaped, before one came to be."[19] Isaiah writes that his vision "has become like the words of a sealed scroll."[20] When God intones to Ezekiel, "Speak my words"[21] to those who have rebelled from his house, he opens his hand, and "in it was a written scroll," which unrolled "before [Ezekiel]; it was covered with writing front and back. Written on it was: Lamentation, wailing, woe!"[22]

The book is the Word; the Word is the book. "The very form of creation is a great book," Augustine writes. "Behold it, examine it, read it from top to bottom. God did not make letters of ink by which you might know him; he set before your eyes the very things that he made."[23] Peter the Venerable, a twelfth-century Benedictine abbot of Cluny, writes that "pages are ploughed by the divine letters and the seed of God's word is planted in the parchment, which ripens into crops of completed books."[24] Books—and their divinely inspired origins—certainly preceded Gutenberg's press, but the speed of production enabled by printing had other, more subtle effects.

"With print," Marshall McLuhan wrote, "the book ceased to be something to be memorized and became a work of reference."[25] During the 1950s, McLuhan collaborated with Edmund Carpenter, a fellow professor at the University of Toronto, to conduct media research. Carpenter taught anthropology courses at the university, but his interests were diverse: he studied Indigenous cultures, worked for the CBC, and examined visual media. McLuhan and Carpenter edited *Explorations*, an experimental communications journal that allowed McLuhan to include his own meandering considerations of television, radio, and language. "I'm making explorations," he would say, appropriately enough, in a later interview. "I don't know where they're going to take me." His books, he claimed, "constitute the process rather than the completed product of discovery." He sought to discover patterns, not data; he promised "to map new terrain rather than chart old landmarks."[26]

Gutenberg's press was another twist in the story of human communication—a route McLuhan thinks reaches back to the time of oral storytelling. Oral storytelling, for McLuhan, stimulated the full imagination. When our ears alone receive the story, our mind offers the story its imagery. The creation of the phonetic alphabet, in contrast, forced our eyes to do the work. Letters and words are not things; they are signs *toward* things. We have become accustomed to such signs, but McLuhan reminds us that our alphabet "dissociates or abstracts, not only sight and sound, but separates all meaning from the sound of the letters, save so far as the meaningless letters relate to the meaningless sounds."[27] McLuhan quotes his one-time student, Walter J. Ong, SJ, who wrote of "how the use of printing moved the word away from its original association with sound and treated it more as a 'thing' in space."[28]

Print is defined by separation in its mechanical production and thereby "fosters a mentality that gradually resists any but a separative and compartmentalizing or specialist outlook."[29] The Gutenberg era, for McLuhan, was the ultimate era of "rapid transition," in which one was stuck "on the frontier between two cultures and between conflicting technologies. Every moment of its consciousness is an act of translation of each of these cultures into the other."[30] The world—and the world of books—was not prepared for the economic and intellectual shift from hand-copied books to mass-produced texts.

McLuhan didn't think the religious nature of the earliest printed books was historical happenstance. "The new homogeneity of the printed page seemed to inspire a subliminal faith in the validity of the printed Bible as bypassing the traditional oral authority of the Church," he argued. The "print, uniform and repeatable" nature of the mass-produced Bible "had the power of creating a new hypnotic superstition of the book as independent of an uncontaminated by human agency."[31] The age of the scribe and the private Mass had given way to a populist faith. Latin gave way to the vernacular. The Bible could be produced in the local tongue. At first, it seemed as if the mass-produced Bible might unite the faith; McLuhan instead concluded that "print is the technology of individualism."[32]

McLuhan's interest in these matters was for a contemporary reason. While those around him looked in awe—and perhaps fear—at the rapidly changing technological world of the 1950s and '60s, McLuhan stepped back in time. The "electronic age," as he called it, followed the "typographic and mechanical era," the results of Gutenberg's innovation. This electronic age was both new—in medium, speed, appearance, and result—and old. It was the return of the oral era, a resurrection of "human interdependence and of expression."[33] No longer were we bound to "visual metaphors and models" of the past centuries; the "electronic pressure of simultaneity" returned us to the oral world.[34]

Print fragmented our senses. The electronic world—radio, television, film—patched us together. Electronic media required that our senses "now constitute a single field of experience which demands that they become collectively conscious."[35] *The Gutenberg Galaxy* offered the backstory for this change; *Understanding Media*, McLuhan's 1964 volume, considered the resulting transfiguration. We are made, and changed, by the mediums through which we communicate.

"Rapidly," McLuhan observed, "we approach the final phase of the extensions of man—the technological simulation of consciousness, when the creative process of knowing will be collectively and corporately extended to the whole of human society, much as we have already extended our senses and our nerves by the various media."[36] The *corpus* of *corporately* here is a spiritual one, for the material world is unable to create or sustain a simultaneous world.

This possible future did not come without risk. McLuhan references Psalm 115:4, "Their idols are silver and gold, the work of human hands." He likens the trouble of our electronic world as similar to the warnings of the psalmist, who "insists that the *beholding* of idols, or the use of technology, conforms men to them."[37] McLuhan, who knew the pliability of language enables us to apply old metaphors to new experiences, found the community and the body to be richly analogous. One of his most famous phrases, *the global village*, is rendered here in a slightly more accurate way: "As electrically contracted, the globe is no more than a village."[38] Electronic communication enables us to unite with anyone, anywhere, and anytime, thus shrinking the world. All business is our business. Simultaneously, in this "electric age we wear all mankind as our skin."[39]

Man and the machine are becoming one, for "in this electric age we see ourselves being translated more and more into the form of information, moving toward the technological extension of consciousness."[40] McLuhan again imbues a religious sense into this transformation: "Might not our current translation of our entire lives into the spiritual form of information seem to make of the entire globe, and of the human family, a single consciousness?"[41] With a nearly dizzying level of prescience, McLuhan, during the early 1960s, was able to conjecture that "computers hold out the promise of a means of instant translation of any code or language into any other code or language."[42]

Prophets divine their wisdom from a source, and one of McLuhan's great inspirations was fellow Catholic Teilhard de Chardin. Teilhard's theories, even in their most radical moments, offered McLuhan a vision for the future. McLuhan embraced the literal and metaphorical symbolism of the book from Gutenberg, and Teilhard showed McLuhan how the electronic word might be made flesh.

Born in 1881, Teilhard earned his geology doctorate at the Sorbonne. He spent more than two decades doing paleontological research in China that influenced his views on evolution. Teilhard wove these scientific views into his theology, resulting in a vision that evolution would continue toward the "Omega Point," at which the universe would evolve toward a final perfection.

"It's not nearly so much ideas that I want to propagate as a spirit," Teilhard writes, "and a spirit can animate all external presentations."[43] In his esoteric statements about cosmology and Christ, Teilhard sought to find divine order in the created world. In 1962, his Jesuit superiors and the

Vatican issued a monitum—a warning—against his writings, asserting that some of his work on original sin contained ambiguous and even erroneous statements about Catholic doctrine. His influence remains, and petitions continue to call for this warning to be removed.

McLuhan's thoughts on Teilhard were not about doctrinal debates; he found in Teilhard a fellow seeker, a writer and thinker whose complex and odd views demanded a new interpretation of our surrounding world. McLuhan was drawn toward one passage in particular from Teilhard's *The Phenomenon of Man*, when the author writes that while the development of the railroad, car, and airplane extended our possibilities for travel, there was a greater power brewing: "Thanks to the prodigious biological event represented by the discovery of electro-magnetic waves, each individual finds himself henceforth (actively and passively) simultaneously present, over land and sea, in every corner of the earth."[44]

The concept—even down to its language—undoubtedly influenced McLuhan's idea of the global village, our instant and continuous global connection through electronics, and yet at points, he sought to distance himself from the Jesuit. In *The Gutenberg Galaxy*, he introduces Teilhard's concept of the noosphere, the priest's idea of a collective human consciousness, as the "lyrical testimony of a very Romantic biologist." McLuhan quips that the idea that a "cosmic membrane that has been snapped round the globe by the electric dilation of our various senses" is "an infantile piece of science fiction."[45]

McLuhan's oddly dismissive tone was part of the general intellectual backlash against Teilhard, whose most eloquent detractor was Father Nogar. "What seems to me to be the basic illusion in his [Teilhard's] vision is this: When Father Teilhard looks out (and inward) upon reality, he sees everything, without exception, as part of an orderly, harmonious whole," Nogar observes.[46] Nogar counters, "[What is] far more obvious to me is the disorder, the waste, the hectic disorganization of the fragments of the universe or reality."[47]

For Nogar, Christ brought that disorder: "Christ reveals Himself as the eccentric, the Lord not of the expected order, but the Lord of the Absurd."[48] His trouble with Teilhard's world "is not that it is strange, but that it is not strange enough." Teilhard's desire "to see all things one, to systematize the cosmos, the life of man, the revelation of God into a blueprint into which everything neatly fits, is far too much like the weakest aspect of contemporary Thomism: the monolithic organon."[49] Teilhard's God was beautiful and symmetric and expansive but distant. The world was not in need of a "God of organization, of chancery decrees and monitums issued from distant places, of manuals and rules, some kind of great scout master. He must be dramatically present among us, now."[50]

McLuhan was likely swayed by such arguments. Yet he was indebted to Teilhard's formulations and would regularly cite his Jesuit predecessor: "The print phrase, however, has encountered today the new organic and biological models of the electronic world. That is, it is now interpenetrated at its extreme development of mechanism by the electrobiological, as de Chardin has explained."[51] He agreed with Teilhard that the electronic age "is not mechanical but organic, and has little sympathy with the values achieved through typography."[52] What McLuhan called the "the Age of Information and of Communication" came from electric media, which "instantly and constantly create a total field of interacting events in which all men participate."[53]

Perhaps the problem was one of tone; Teilhard could be read as an optimistic voice about the evolution of the universe, while McLuhan was more inclined toward disorder and skepticism. McLuhan felt uneasy about the electronic world, particularly the sense-dizzying power of television. McLuhan would not be the last scholar to muddy his influences for fear they lessened his novelty. Years later, McLuhan and Teilhard would often be mentioned in tandem for their prophetic insights. *Wired* magazine, the pioneering publication of digital life, named Marshall McLuhan as their patron saint. They also devoted a feature story in their June 1995 issue to Teilhard, "whose quirky philosophy points, oddly, right into cyberspace."[54]

The spirit of Teilhard's vision certainly encapsulates a creative interpretation of the electronic world and helped give language to McLuhan's own theories, but his ideas require some transference before they help describe our world. Teilhard largely predated the electronic age, but his interest was in an omnipresent evolutionary sense—not a technological one. McLuhan, in contrast, lived and was sustained by the electric age. His theories, even at their most ambitious, were grounded in the budding circuitry that surrounded him. McLuhan pondered the future but couldn't help returning to the past.

Gutenberg was the perfect locus for McLuhan. Gutenberg didn't invent the concept of print; he synthesized the elements of print necessary for mass production. McLuhan didn't invent the electronic world, and neither was he the first to comment on it—but he was one of the best at attempting to trace its influences, routes, and results. More than anything, Gutenberg represented for McLuhan a pivot point in the history of writing, communication, and our conception of the book. McLuhan posited that Gutenberg's printing press "was the first important step in the process of accelerating relations between people."[55] "It was the Gutenberg method of homogeneous segmentation," McLuhan wrote, "for which centuries of phonetic literacy had prepared the psychological ground, that evoked the traits of the modern world." The "events and products of that method of mechanization of handicrafts"— the message of that medium—was "merely incidental to the method itself."[56] McLuhan's route toward this point is a mixture of revelations and coincidences. Like most prophets, McLuhan became one through a fascination with God.

2

A New Form
of Expression

"It is wonderful to go out into empty streets—they are very narrow and not too crooked—and hear great bells striking solemnly all about you," McLuhan wrote of his time studying at Cambridge.[1] His life there was busy with "rowing, teas, halls, and lectures morning and evening," and he marveled at how "it is amazing what one can do in a buoyant mood."[2] "Certainly I have no right to be as fortunate and happy," he wrote to his family, "but shall probably have enough of thin times hereafter to level up so that I shall die neither more or less felicitous than common men."[3]

McLuhan's years at Cambridge were the most formative in his life. There he became established as a traveler, an itinerant preacher of the electronic age, whose distance from his native Canada helped him develop his perceptive sense—especially attuned to how cultural assumptions formed and sometimes stunted thought. He converted to Catholicism, concluding an emotional and academic journey that replaced the anodyne faith of his youth with a fervent, mysterious belief that offered supple metaphors for understanding the world. He read deeply and widely in the literature of the early Church, an especially fraught era when faith and secular power clashed. He found two Catholic touchstones that would offer him intellectual anchors for the rest of his life: Gerard Manley Hopkins and James Joyce.

McLuhan thought Hopkins's syntax transcended the English of his time. A radical stylist with earnest faith, Hopkins's poetic sense of inscape enabled him to revise conventional ideas about language. McLuhan posited that Hopkins was the essential point in a literary evolution that began with Baudelaire and Rimbaud and ended with Joyce: the recognition that language is not merely an "environment" of communication but a "probe" and "instrument of exploration and research."[4]

McLuhan's preferred mode of communication was the mosaic: discrete and succinct observations and references, which were "not uniform, continuous, or repetitive" but instead "discontinuous, skew, and nonlinear, like the tactual TV image."[5] McLuhan conceived of television as a palpable medium, one that projected its image onto the audience. In language appropriated from Hopkins, McLuhan considered touch the most alive of all senses, for with touch, "all things are sudden, counter, original, spare, strange." Hopkins's poem "Pied Beauty" was a "catalogue of the notes of the sense of touch," a "manifesto of the nonvisual, and like Cezanne or Seurat, or Rouault it provides an indispensable approach to understanding TV."[6] A nineteenth-century Victorian Jesuit priest can help us understand mid-twentieth-century media: a paradoxical claim, but as with much of McLuhan's thought, his paradoxes soon became viable prophecies.

For McLuhan, there was no greater modern inheritor of complex stylistics and paradoxes than James Joyce—a writer whose latent Catholicism and Jesuit instruction created the perfect synthesis of word and the Word. "Irremediably analogical," McLuhan wrote, "Joyce's work moves as naturally on the metaphysical as on the naturalistic plane."[7] McLuhan thought Joyce had "devised a new form of expression" that prefigured the electronic and digital modes of communication.[8]

McLuhan arrived at his full appreciation for Joyce through his work at Cambridge. In 1943, McLuhan received his PhD there, completing a dissertation titled "The Place of Thomas Nashe in the Learning of His Time." An Elizabethan satirist known for play and provocation, Nashe might seem like an odd choice for a scholar who would soon become interested in the electronic world. But McLuhan was drawn toward linguistic dissenters—those who ruptured the conventional idea of what language, syntax, and communication might accomplish. "The oral polyphony of the prose of Nashe offends against lineal and literary decorum," McLuhan noted.[9] McLuhan, a recent convert to Catholicism, drawn to the Trinity and all of its symbolic possibilities, examined the "classical trivium" of grammar, dialectic, and rhetoric in the work of Nashe, a precedent for his later focus on the *medium* as the *message*.

McLuhan's history of the trivium from Augustine to Nashe takes up more than three-fourths of his Cambridge dissertation. In this context, McLuhan intends grammar to reference the action of interpretation, a practice that might begin with literary works but could be used for other texts and even everyday situations. The dialectic is a method of testing evidence—for purposes of argument, dialogue, or thinking. Rhetoric includes both the methods of persuasion and related devices of language but also the process from concept to presentation. His dissertation employs a methodical, comprehensive approach, the work of a research project and not a book meant for wide distribution. Yet if we meet McLuhan at the goals of his intended project, we find a skeleton key for his later works.

By examining the classical trivium, McLuhan could argue that how we write—technique, structure, elements—influences how we perceive, and vice versa. Although he would later move on from the classical trivium to the contemporary electronic mode of communication, McLuhan retained his appreciation for the methods of the trivium and therefore approached the modern world with an ancient foundation.

McLuhan's tendency to seek *timeless* concepts with which to deconstruct *timely* concerns is revealed in the breadth of his dissertation, a work that bubbles with metaphors that he would later apply to the electronic world. Early in the dissertation, he references Genesis 2:19, Adam's knowledge of naming all things. McLuhan claims that the "business of art is, however, to recover the knowledge of that language which once man held by nature."[10] He envisions the recovery of essential knowledge as a long tradition, one that reaches from "the time of the neo-Platonists and Augustine to Bonaventura and to Francis Bacon" and for which "the art of grammar provided not only the sixteenth-century approach to the Book of Life in scriptural exegesis but to the Book of Nature, as well."[11]

In McLuhan's vision of the classical trivium, words themselves "condense and translate the most ancient effect of things upon us."[12] McLuhan returns to Francis Bacon's idea of the aphorism as the core of thought. Bacon surmised that while our thoughts become "further polished" as we become more erudite and stylistic in an attempt to present those thoughts to an audience, our original ideas "increaseth no more in bulk and substance."[13] Bacon was concerned more with medium than message. "Aphorisms," he argued, "representing a knowledge broken, do invite men to inquire farther; whereas Methods, carrying the show of a total, do secure men, as if they were at farthest."[14]

McLuhan's iterations of the aphorism were his probes and mosaics. As a Catholic, McLuhan believed that the world is full of mysteries and complexities, and therefore knowledge is an action of searching. We seek, we probe, we hypothesize, and we recognize that we often fail. Polished sentences and learned syntaxes can trick us into thinking that stylistic writing equals intellectual certainty, but McLuhan felt such an approach stymied inquiry.

The final quarter of his dissertation is focused on Thomas Nashe, a jocular stylist whose work ranged from the profound to the profane. McLuhan considered Nashe a "test-case" for his examination of the classical trivium:

"If a writer so admittedly eccentric and original can be shown to be capable of becoming best understood in light of the foregoing study, then its usefulness for understanding other writers of the same period may very reasonably be granted."[15] It is notable that McLuhan chose a pugilistic satirist for whom language is pliable and nearly poisonous as his test for the limits of language.

Nashe, McLuhan was careful to note, "had a definite philosophy of rhetoric and a precise notion of its function in the society of his day." His flourishes were focused, not fevered. He would sometimes employ a "grand style in conjunction with low images," but this juxtaposition was for clear rhetorical intent. Nashe knowingly participated in a tradition of "great patristic exemplars."[16] Hyperbole, paradox, prosopopoeia: Nashe used the highest style but also famously quipped, "I prostitute my pen in hope of gaine."[17]

McLuhan accomplishes the goal of his study, but in its final pages, he teases an interesting nugget: "It required, perhaps, the advent of such a successful devotee of the second sophistic as James Joyce, to prepare the ground for a scholarly understanding of Elizabethan literature."[18] The dissertation ends without further development of the point, but we get the sense that McLuhan recognized his historical study would compel him to turn his attention toward more contemporary concerns. However interesting, Nashe is a minor writer—yet often minor writers are the most potent pivots in literary history.

McLuhan converted to Catholicism during his dissertation work. There was certainly an emotional element to his arrival at the faith, but his research syllabus is instructive: McLuhan was reading patristic writing, the Bible, Thomas Nashe, James Joyce, G. K. Chesterton, and Gerard Manley Hopkins. He was reading writers steeped in Catholicism—or, in the case of Nashe, the kind who could pivot from a ribald to an Anglican apologia. Earnestness and satire were read in tandem. Although varied in subject and style, writing in satirical and apologetic modes often employed some measure of affect in order to accomplish rhetorical goals. The medium and its delivery were essential.

Nashe turns out to have been an apt choice for the conclusion of a dissertation on classical rhetoric. As the critic Alan Jacobs observes, those of Nashe's time "near the beginning of the age of print, in a London raucous with ballads, playhouses, and pamphleteers, were people who were at one and the same time thoroughly classical and utterly contemporary."[19] An even more contemporary version of this synthesis was James Joyce.

Linearity was pleasantly logical, but life and even God, as Father Nogar argued, are absurd. The patterns that we think we find in nature might be arrangements of our own doing as we project onto the world a comforting order. In novels like *Ulysses* and *Finnegans Wake*, Joyce rejects the traditional linearity of print narratives. The page, perhaps, was our prison. The arrival of "electric media released art" from the "straitjacket" of print, "creating the world of Paul Klee, Picasso, Braque, Eisenstein, the Marx Brothers, and James Joyce."[20]

"McLuhan, at times, does talk like a character that Joyce might have created," quipped the *Washington Post*'s television critic in 1966, when McLuhan seemed to be everywhere with an opinion about everything.[21] The observation is not without merit. McLuhan was at his most provocative when the medium of language demanded it, and Joyce was a formidable model. Although McLuhan acknowledged that Joyce was not "a model Catholic," he observed that secular appreciation of the Irish novelist's "genius and art" was "unthinkable apart from his immersion in the traditions of Catholic theology and philosophy."[22] A complex thinker whose complexities were generated by—and perhaps sustained by—Catholic theology, Joyce was not long for belief, but Irish Catholicism is as much a culture and worldview as it is a religion, and his absence of practice might have made his literary Catholicism even more acute. Joyce did not rely on a shared belief with his audience, so his portrayal of Catholicism in his short stories and novels is especially textured and developed.

From the start, Joyce stimulated McLuhan's imagination: "A bit startled to note last page of Finnegan is a rendering of the last part of the Mass. Remembered that opening of Ulysses is from 1st words of the Mass. The whole thing an intellectual Black Mass."[23] After reading an essay about "Joyce's esthetic doctrine of the *epiphany*" in the Summer 1946 issue of *Sewanee Review*, McLuhan thought the concept was the "same as Hopkins' *inscape*."[24] Joyce defined his vision of epiphany as "the gropings of a spiritual eye which seeks to adjust its vision to an exact focus."[25] Prose-poetic vignettes, his epiphanies suggested that life was a series of sharp, disparate moments. Joyce's epiphanies were both structure and subject, medium and message. In both his epiphanies and his full-length works, Joyce appeared to suggest that profluent narratives were a literary desire rather than a reflection of actual existence, during which dry spells and spikes of joy invade our daily tedium.

Nashe was a curious footnote for McLuhan, a "Cambridge pet." Joyce was the Catholic alchemist mystic that McLuhan needed; his study of media "began and remain[ed] rooted" in the Irish novelist.[26] Joyce was the great disruptor. McLuhan would often observe that the layout of a newspaper—the "jazzy, ragtime discontinuity of press items"—seemed more like a piece of modern art than a coherent arrangement, and he claimed that discontinuity is "the literary technique of James Joyce."[27] Joyce's *Ulysses* spurred artists across genres to see "that there was a new art form of universal scope present in the technical layout of the modern newspaper." Rather than a "superficial chaos," the patchwork arrangement of the front page was the ultimate medium of the masses.[28]

Joyce, "who took an intelligent interest in everybody and everything," embraced "the ads, the comics, the pulps, and popular speech," funneling them through the classical education he received from the Jesuits at Clongowes, Belvedere, and University College, Dublin.[29] Joyce had studied the classical trivium that was at the center of McLuhan's expansive dissertation, and his instruction in the "traditional arts of communication" was delivered within a theologically rich setting.[30] McLuhan interpreted the Aeolus episode of *Ulysses*—set in the office of a Dublin newspaper—as Joyce "[breaking] open the closed system of classical rhetoric at the same time that he cuts into the closed system of newspaper somnambulism."[31] He "saw the parallels, on one hand, between the modern frontier of the verbal and the pictorial and, on the other, between the Homeric world poised between the old sacral culture and the new profane or literate sensibility."[32] Joyce was a man of transition, and his Leopold Bloom, wandering around Dublin during a day that felt like all eternity, is a character who unites the past and the present.

Both McLuhan and Joyce were interested in how visual media reconfigured narrative and communication. In 1909, several years before he started writing *Ulysses*, Joyce opened Ireland's "first permanent cinema, the Volta" in Dublin.[33] He worked with several investors to start the business, and while it seems to have been more of an economic venture than a purely artistic pursuit, Joyce was fascinated with film. The interest preceded cinema proper: Joyce was drawn to visual representation and fragmentation. His fiction abounds with references to "optical toys, shadowgraphy, magic lanternism, panoramas, dioramas, rapid photography and peepshows based on Edison's Kinetoscope"—including emulations of these "imagistic" movements within his sentences.[34]

Upon reading the serialized version of Joyce's *Ulysses* in 1918, Virginia Woolf wrote that his story was "like a cinema that shows you very slowly, how a horse does jump" and "all the pictures were a little made up before. Here is thought made phonetic—taken to bits." Joyce was able to represent "both phenomenon observed *and* the subject perceiving and reflecting on it."[35] This is essentially Hopkins's conception of inscape: how all things have a unique proportion and presence, one that is literal but also spiritual. Perhaps the perfect form of writing is that which supplants the actual experience—that transcends what our senses can observe during the real moment. There is a liturgical, ritual sense to this transformation, and that process would not be lost on a student of the Jesuits, where God is seen in all things.

Keith B. Williams finds this method first occurring in Joyce's 1904 version of what would become *A Portrait of the Artist as a Young Man*: "a means for figuring both physical and psychological motion to present the rhythm of a consciousness developing over time equivalent to the way rapid photography (feeding into cinema) dissected and recomposed living motion."[36] Joyce's personal interest in film and his temporary participation in the economy of cinema lend credence to this hypothesis.

His novels—down to their sentences—feel imbued with a modern sense of inscape. In the Proteus chapter of *Ulysses*, Stephen Dedalus walks along Sandymount strand: "Stephen closed his eyes to hear his boots crush crackling wrack and shells. You are walking through it howsomever. I am, a stride at a time."[37] A cinematic, hypnotic feel carries these sentences: the eyes closing, sound replacing sight, the sharp "crackling" linked in letter and sound to "wrack," creating a strong pop before "shells." Joyce slips second-person perspective into the next sentence, putting us physically into the scene in which we have already experienced as a mere reader and then completing the transition with the teasingly Christological "I am," followed by the implication that Stephen's body *is* its motion. No wonder McLuhan found Joyce to be downright liturgical.

A later paragraph in the same chapter further captures what Woolf thought transformative about Joyce's method. Stephen notices a couple's loose dog, which "ambled about a bank of dwindling sand, trotting, sniffing on all sides." The dog is constantly profluent, and Joyce's syntax participates in the shifts—his commas working like the dog's fluttering hair in the wind. An abrupt and mysterious interjection—"Looking for something lost in a past life"—is perfectly in place with the feeling of an aimless, ethereal walk on the beach. The dog then bounds, "ears flung back, chasing the shadow of a lowskimming gull," stopped only when his owner's "shrieked whistle struck his limp ears." What follows feels like Hopkins: "He turned, bounded back, came nearer, trotted on twinkling shanks. On a field tenney a buck, trippant, proper, unattired. At the lacefringe of the tide he halted with stiff forehoofs, seawardpointed ears. His snout lifted barked at the wavenoise, herds of seamorse. They serpented towards his feet, curling, unfurling many crests, every ninth, breaking, plashing, from far, from farther out, waves and waves."[38] Joyce's sentences are but words on a page, but their result is multimodal.

We might return to Woolf's praise of Joyce's language as "thought made phonetic"—even though Joyce was describing an animal's action that neither he nor the narrator nor Stephen could understand internally. The inscape of the scene is that the action and the perception of the action are perfectly described; in a way, the dog is moved by being perceived by Stephen. The section is best read aloud in the same manner that McLuhan thought Hopkins should also be spoken: "The words the reader sees are not the words that he will hear."[39]

In a similar way, the Catholic Mass in Latin—which Joyce, no longer fully believing, rarely participated in except during Holy Saturday yet retained a vestigial attraction to—encapsulated the syncopation in Joyce's sentences and even Hopkins's poetic lines. Joyce and Hopkins did not merely represent reality; they re-created it and in doing so affirmed language as essential and sacred rather than merely a means of communication. This appealed to McLuhan on an artistic level as well as a spiritual one. Joyce, especially, dramatized "the metamorphoses of the sacred in such an era of technologization," as McLuhan's University of Toronto colleague Donald F. Theall surmised.[40] Joyce was a sentimental Catholic by virtue of his distance-borne nostalgia; to call him a lapsed Catholic correctly implies a falling away from faith rather than a simple severing of belief—for a Catholic so deeply reared in the faith feels the pull, even against dogmatic skepticism.

Joyce's participation within a time of cultural and technological transition mirrored McLuhan's own context. His fiction offered "the ground for new modes of ritual and sacrifice."[41] Ever the sentimental satirist, Joyce asked his brother Stanislaus if "there is a certain resemblance between the mystery of the Mass and what I am trying to do?"[42] *Finnegans Wake* abounds with references to and subversions of the Easter Triduum, including the washing of the feet and the lighting of the paschal candle.[43] *Ulysses* and *Finnegans Wake* might be considered the technologically conscious evolution of the final pages of *A Portrait of the Artist as a Young Man*: that a man rejecting his religion and country becomes that man rejecting the technology of the past.

Finnegans Wake became McLuhan's prototext because, as Theall observes, it was "one of the first major poetic encounters with the challenge that electronic media present to the traditionally accepted relationships between speech, script and print."[44] McLuhan was especially drawn to *Finnegans Wake* and conjectured that "as the alphabet ends its cycle we move out of visual space into discontinuous auditory space again."[45] Joyce's notoriously inscrutable text was, for McLuhan, actually a deeply revelatory vision of a writer who concluded that traditional narrative and communication were inadequate for stories of our modern world. The novel was "a great intellectual effort aimed at rinsing the Augean stables of speech and society with geysers of laughter."[46]

Torn between our personal, private visions and the feeling that we have a tribal identity, McLuhan thought we might find "liberation from the dilemma" through "the new electric technology, with its profound organic character. For the electric puts the mythic or collective dimension of human experience fully into the conscious" and everyday world.[47] Raised on the classical trivium, Joyce was influenced by the French symbolist poets, whose *vers libre* was not arbitrary but instead "a return to the formal rhythms of early litanies, hymns, and to the psalter."[48] Among them, Stéphane Mallarmé especially offered Joyce a view "of language as gesture, as efficacious, and as representing a total human response," so that what seemed like rigid rules of grammar and method were instead revelations of what it meant to be human. Mallarmé's views of language, McLuhan thought, were "familiar to the Church Fathers, and underlay the major schools of scriptural exegesis."[49]

In the end, what made Hopkins and Joyce especially apt for McLuhan was their Catholicism. The two were not similar Catholics. Hopkins was drawn to the wilderness, where he cultivated an earnest faith supplanted with a melancholy sense. Joyce was drawn to the circuit-like road-ways of urban life; his writing became a form of religious practice. Hopkins was an actual Jesuit; Joyce once quipped, "You allude to me as a Catholic. Now for the sake of precision and to get the correct contour on me, you ought to allude to me as a Jesuit."[50]

McLuhan notes that everything Joyce wrote carried a "liturgical level," a spiritual "dimension" that enabled Joyce "to manipulate such encyclopedic lore, guided by his analogical awareness of liturgy as both an order of knowledge and an order of grace."[51] In the same way that Hopkins, Baudelaire, and other Catholic poets used language to transform reality rather than merely communicate experience, Joyce sought the "submerged metaphysical drama" of language. In that place, Joyce could play: the "quirks, 'slips,' and freaks of ordinary discourse" enabled him "to evoke the fullness of existence in speech."[52] Again, here was Joyce mirroring the Catholic literary art of a writer as different as Chesterton, who similarly used "the pun as a way of seeing the paradoxical exuberance of being through language."[53] McLuhan was nourished by these Catholic antecedents.

Joyce, living on the precipice of mechanical and technical change, became McLuhan's literary guide. Joyce's particular gift was his recognition of the paradox that language, while pliable, often fell short of actual experience—and yet certain turns of phrase feel more beautiful than reality itself. The tension sounds like an impossible task for writers, but Joyce's Catholicism prepared him well. Writing in the French experimental literary magazine *Transitions* in 1927, the poet William Carlos Williams observes that Joyce's style was uniquely powerful: "his broken words, the universality of his growing language which is no longer english." Contrary to the provincial readings of Joyce that imagine him to be exclusively Irish, Williams argues that Joyce's language "has no faculties of place." Joyce included "German, French, Italian, Latin, Irish, anything"—resulting in a transformation: "Time and space do not exist, it is all one in the eyes of God—and man."[54]

None more than McLuhan would appreciate such synthesis: a literary transubstantiation, perhaps. "For me, the model of the turned-on, tuned-in, dropped-out man is James Joyce, the great psychedelic writer of this century," wrote Timothy Leary—the Jesuit-educated, Irish Catholic psychologist-guru—in 1967. Delivering a literary allusion that revealed his appreciation for *Finnegans Wake*, Leary said that Joyce "pour[ed] out a river-run of pun, jest, put-on, up-level, comic word acrobatics," before concluding, "The impact of Joyce via McLuhan on the psychedelic age cannot be overestimated."[55] According to Leary, it was McLuhan himself who offered Leary's iconic, almost vaguely Trinitarian-rhythmic phrase "Turn on, tune in, drop out."[56] Joyce and McLuhan, however different in background and experiences, shared an eccentric, deeply Catholic vision that informed their understanding of communication and popular culture.

Years after Cambridge, when he was traveling as a prophet of the electronic age, McLuhan was examining a world that was unfinished and contradictory. Some wanted to stop the coming electronic era, while others just watched it happen. For decades, radios had blared news, music, and stories. By 1962, nine out of ten American homes had a television.[57] The first issue of *Computerworld*, claiming to be the "first newspaper for the full computer community," launched in June 1967.[58] McLuhan documented technological changes, examined them, and wondered how they might change us: our identities, our modes of communication, our humanity. Bacon's example of a thinker who has pondered himself into certainty is unprepared to examine a changing world. Only a fragmented approach could engage the electronic world. While Hopkins and Joyce were revelatory precedents for McLuhan, like them, he needed to encounter his own era. Steeped in literary and religious history, steeled by faith, and charged with an open and omnivorous mind, McLuhan was ready to take on his electronic present.

3

The Coming
Electronic Communion

A comedian and an elocutionist in a converted cow barn: sounds more like the setup for a joke than an event that would transform communication. On April 7, 1927, in Whippany, New Jersey, engineers at Bell Laboratories frantically checked connections for an important public demonstration. The company had purchased the property—nearly forty acres of farmland—the year before as its location for experimental radio work, which would later turn into military research. But on this spring morning, the engineers were attempting to replicate something that had been depicted in the recently released science fiction film *Metropolis*: they hoped to demonstrate that television could become a reality.

An eager crowd of business executives, bankers, editors, and influential members of the media congregated in New York City to watch video broadcasts from two locations. First, they heard from future president Herbert Hoover, who was then the Secretary of Commerce. Hoover had a particular penchant for radio, but on this day his image was sent by wire "on a screen as motion pictures" from Washington DC.[1] Hoover's speech from the nation's capital was appropriately optimistic: "All we can say today is that there has been created a marvelous agency for whatever use the future may find, with the full realization that every great and fundamental discovery of the past has been followed by use far beyond the vision of its creator."[2]

Hoover's grand address was rather unceremoniously followed by a second broadcast: a vaudeville performance in Whippany. A local comedian by the name of A. F. Dolan mimicked "a stage Irishman, with side whiskers and a broken pipe, and did a monologue in brogue" before breaking into a caricatured portrayal of Black vernacular.[3] Video of Dolan's ethnic stereotypes and racial minstrel have thankfully been lost to history—an eerily appropriate example of when the medium far exceeds the message.

Dolan was followed by "a short humorous dialect talk" by Celina Bouquet Frederick, a local performer whose husband, Halsey A. Frederick, was director of Transmission Instruments Development at the laboratory and who led the development of the company's handset telephone.[4] Although Frederick was not involved in the television transmission—an engineer named E. L. Nelson explained the new process—his role at the laboratory would have made him aware of the novel event, and perhaps his wife's talents were volunteered.

Either way, the engineers in Whippany thought that a presentation of *art* through performance would be more appropriate, or perhaps compelling, for this pivotal moment than merely a speech. "Here then was a practical achievement of the television dream," wrote the editors of *Bell Laboratories Record*, "sight and sound transmitted simultaneously by radio for the enjoyment of a distant audience."[5] Around the same time as the Whippany broadcast, the elocutionist Elsie Naomi Hall McLuhan was performing often in Winnipeg, as well as traveling to "Toronto, Minneapolis and St. Paul." Billed as a "Reader and Impersonator," she performed scenes from contemporary and classic literature, plays, and character sketches of similar subject and style as Celina Frederick in Whippany.[6]

Elsie McLuhan would often bring her sons Marshall and Maurice on her performance trips. Although young Marshall was likely unaware of the nearly miraculous transmission that bounded from Whippany to New York and Washington DC—a medium that would later consume much of his intellectual life—at that moment, he was observing his mother perform language for an audience. In much the same way as McLuhan would later examine the transfiguration of language that occurred during the ritual of Mass, young McLuhan was exposed to a performative world of language through his mother. Her elocution revealed the "mutability" of words to him, how words could "morph and change texture on the tongue."[7]

Playfulness and performance: a synthesis that enabled Elsie McLuhan to take on other identities and enabled Marshall McLuhan to share his theories with the world. "I don't explain," McLuhan assured of his own speeches, "I explore."[8]

Beginning in the 1950s, McLuhan turned his exploration and attention toward the budding and befuddling electronic age. For McLuhan, mass media was a form of Mass. When we communicate electronically, not only do we send information; we send ourselves. This extension, and the corresponding receipt and perception, creates a changed environment for all involved: a transformation of almost sacred power. In a series of essays, books, and television appearances, McLuhan developed a complex, evolving vision of the electronic world. He was a self-identified seeker, as he was in the *midst* of a change. His cultural analysis began with *The Mechanical Bride: Folklore of Industrial Man* (1951), in which he examined the mass communication of print advertising—a meticulous, obsessive documentation of the advertising "trance," which "seems to be what perpetuates the widely occurring cluster image of sex, technology, and death which constitutes the mystery of the mechanical bride."[9] This trance—hypnotic, ecstatic, vaguely *religious*—was perfected in television, during which the viewer was christened: "Information pours upon us, instantaneously and continuously."[10] In the spirit of *The Medium Is the Massage* (1967), McLuhan forwards a radical theory of electronic media—completing the evolution from spoken word to moveable type to mass production to immediate, worldwide electronic communion. McLuhan rode these changes because he was playfully bombastic and anchored with the confidence of one who earnestly believes that God's mysteries are the foundation and fire of this world.

The path from elocution to television, from performed speech to projected image, is a direct one. McLuhan's mother, who was trained by graduates of the renowned

Emerson College of Oratory, took everyday language and bent and blurred it through appropriated identity. Speaking before her son and the others in the audience, she was both herself and not—a refraction of herself, perhaps. It is a fitting metaphor to help us understand the medium of television, one that McLuhan would envision as a terrible and miraculous gift to the world.

The 1927 Bell Labs television presentation was a media success, with the *New York Times* devoting multiple stories to the event. Any new medium challenges language. One writer attempted to describe the new process of transmitting an image across a distance: "The face is optically sliced into thousands of fragments of light and shade. An 'eye' or photoelectric cell sees each fragment and converts it into an electric impulse," and then at the receiving end, "the electric impulses are reconverted into optical fragments correctly assembled and corresponding in light-value and position with the originals."[11] Television, like language, disrupts and then reconnects image and idea. Much like the stylistic lines and sentences of Gerard Manley Hopkins and James Joyce, television was a new form of communication.

In that first transmission, art and language coalesced to create a dizzying new reality. The process is familiar to how the poet W. B. Yeats imagined the language of poetry. Ever the mystic, Yeats thought the symbolism of poetry arose from "disembodied powers, whose footsteps over our hearts we call emotions."[12] These existing associations, many of which we are not consciously aware of, are often stirred by the lyric arts. Once conjured, poetry "grows more powerful, it flows out, with all it has gathered, among the blind instincts of daily life, where it moves a power within powers, as one sees ring within ring in the stem of an old tree."[13]

Yeats certainly thought that such artistic alchemy was present in poetry, but not exclusively so. A participant in the late nineteenth-century spiritual practice of theosophy, Yeats was drawn to an esoteric conception of God. Yeats participated in séances and famously generated substantial material through the automatic writing of his wife, Georgie Hyde-Lees. Poetic symbolism was the most authentic presentation of human emotion, and that symbolism arose in trance. In "The Symbolism of Poetry," Yeats argued that the purpose of rhythm was "to prolong the moment of contemplation, the moment when we are both asleep and awake, which is the one moment of creation."[14]

Rhythm, produced through ritual, quiets "us with an alluring monotony, while it holds us waking by variety," and in that trance, "the mind liberated from the pressure of the will is unfolded in symbols." Written two decades before the first television transmission, Yeats's language captures the projection of screen to viewer. He writes of how some may be entranced by keeping their "gaze persistently on the monotonous flashing of a light."[15] The artist creates patterns, which "are but the monotonous flash woven to take the eyes in a subtler enchantment."[16] The "making" and "understanding" of art, "full of patterns and symbols and music," may lure us "to the threshold of sleep."[17]

Yeats's description of this experience mirrors McLuhan's vision of the hypnotic powers of advertising and television as languages and media. In one of his early literary essays for the *Sewanee Review*, McLuhan includes a section from Yeats's autobiography *The Trembling of the Veil* titled "Hodos Camelionis." Yeats posits that certain unspoken thoughts may "pass into the general mind" and that a nation is "bound together by this interchange among streams or shadows." Any nation and culture is sustained by "that invisible commerce of reverie and of sleep"—a curiously apt language and sentiment for McLuhan to quote in a broader essay about Southern American literature.[18]

McLuhan praises Yeats's search for an animating and uniting symbol of Irish culture: "Yeats passionately and humbly sets himself to watch and listen for the hints and promptings of a corporate wisdom far richer than his merely individual perception can invent."[19] This communion, to follow Yeats's vision, is created and sustained through a state of language and self that is steeped in symbol. McLuhan returns to this Yeatsian concept in his 1970 book, *From Cliché to Archetype*. Early in the book, he uses a poem by Yeats, "The Circus Animals' Desertion," to establish the elasticity of language. Yeats writes, "Those masterful images because complete / Grew in pure mind, but out of what began? / A mound of refuse or the sweepings of a street, / Old kettles, old bottles, and a broken can." Language arises from the detritus among us, our need to document and describe. "The most masterful images," McLuhan writes, "when complete, are tossed aside and the process begins anew." As Yeats describes, "Now that my ladder's gone, / I must lie down where all the ladders start, / In the foul rag-and-bone shop of the heart." McLuhan goes so far as to say that Yeats's single poem encapsulates the theme of his entire book.[20]

"Yeats assumes," McLuhan reminds us, "that sleep is a process of purging the images of the day by a *ricorso*, or rehearsal, such as constitutes the entire action of *Finnegans Wake*."[21] Since McLuhan thought Joyce's novel was an attempt to renew the English language in a single narrative night, his interest in Yeats is fitting. Later in the book, McLuhan says that Yeats's "entire creative procedure" is concerned with "classifying" the "rejected fragments of obsolete and broken cultures," since "new cliches or new technological probes and environments have the effect of liquidating or scrapping the preceding cliches of cultures and environments created by preceding technologies."[22] Like Joyce, Yeats was able to channel "myth, in manipulating a continuous parallel between contemporaneity and antiquity"—but McLuhan is clear that Yeats was "the first contemporary to be conscious" of this method.[23]

Symbol, pattern, rhetoric, and "resonance and repetition": that which lures us into a sleep state makes us persuadable.[24] McLuhan thought advertising and television were the two great sleep-trances of popular culture, and even his rendering of Yeats's influence is colored by this interpretation. Yeats often told the story about how one of his most famous poems, "The Lake Isle of Innisfree," was inspired by a shop window advertisement for a drink. In Yeats's telling, the image of "a little jet of water balancing a ball on the top . . . set me thinking of Sligo and lake water." Essentially, the advertisement recalled Yeats's desire to, like Thoreau, "live in a hut on an island."[25]

In McLuhan's telling, "While Yeats stood on the pavement in the eye-, ear-, and air-polluted metropolis" of London, "he proceeded to create an anti-environment, namely 'innisfree,' in order to make sense of the anarchy of the world around him."[26] Less interesting to McLuhan is the reflection of Yeats's youthful desire for a wilderness escape; rather, McLuhan uses the anecdote to probe how an advertisement was generative for the artist—even if the result was different from its original intention. Ad-speak surrounds us, McLuhan demonstrates, so we must engage its language.

McLuhan did just that in *The Mechanical Bride*, which is best considered as his initial attempt to understand how mass communication alters meaning and experience. McLuhan focused on print advertisements; his first book was firmly in the mechanical world and not the electronic one. In his preface, McLuhan strikes what seems like a paranoid tone as he explains that some of the best-trained minds of his day are working to "manipulate, exploit, control" the "collective public mind" and to "keep everybody in the helpless state engendered by prolonged mental rutting." In such a world, McLuhan argues, we need to mimic the main character of "A Descent into the Maelstrom" by Edgar Allan Poe: "Poe's sailor saved himself by studying the action of the whirlpool and by co-operating with it." McLuhan knew that we could not change the information and advertising age; we had to learn to observe it, understand it, move with it. He quotes Poe's sailor to establish his true tone for the book: "I must have been delirious, for I even sought amusement in speculating upon the relative velocities of their several descents toward the foam below."[27]

Perhaps channeling the Thomas Nashe of his dissertation, McLuhan embraces a spirit of amusement: "Many who are accustomed to the note of moral indignation will mistake this amusement for mere indifference."[28] The only way for McLuhan to take the advertising world seriously is by approaching it with amusement and play; he is remaining nimble when anger would render him stolid. What follows are a series of short essays that deconstruct contemporary print advertisements, a side effect of his early university teaching. McLuhan's first teaching position at the University of Wisconsin forced him to realize that theories of pedagogy meant little compared to the reality of the classroom. His Cambridge-born literary erudition wouldn't fly with his young students, who "spoke in slang, knew little of history and almost nothing of the cultures of the past."[29]

These students, as Douglas Coupland notes, "lived in a perpetual present and saw nothing wrong with that." McLuhan had to adjust; he had to enter their world of "mass culture" and, in doing so, was thrown into the ancillary world of advertising.[30] McLuhan's plunge into this world made him, Coupland writes, "arguably the first person on earth to be a metacritic . . . *The Mechanical Bride* marks both the end of McLuhan's focus on content and the beginning of his movement away from what was being said to *how* it was being said; to the ways in which content is put forth into the world."[31] He fashioned himself, in the tradition of Joyce, as one who "refused to be distracted by the fashion-conscious sirens of content and subject matter and proceeded straight to the utilization of the universal forms of the artistic process itself."[32] "Our world," McLuhan writes, "of mechanized routines, abstract finance and engineering is the consolidated dream born of a wish," and by "studying the dream in our folklore, we can, perhaps, find the clue to understanding and guiding our world in more reasonable courses."[33] Even in his first book, McLuhan sought to understand the structure of our communication, knowing that its artifice was far more important than its content.

This framing turned out to be a perfect one for McLuhan, who could somehow both take himself too seriously and pun at the level of a master satirist. The aphorism in the form of a mosaic was his perfect medium because its brevity implied importance, while its awareness of sound and play suggested that McLuhan had internalized the cadence of advertising while turning it into a mode of criticism.

Generations later, many of the advertisements that McLuhan examines appear equal parts trite and absurd— but his analysis remains creative. In an advertisement for Palomino, "the stocking color that will sweep you into Spring '47," a well-dressed woman stands against one side of a stone arch. Her gloved hands, crossed, hold a purse. Behind her, in the white background, is a rearing stallion. McLuhan suggests a Picasso-like technique of juxtaposition here, while also invoking references to *Madame Bovary* and A. N. Whitehead's *Science and the Modern World*. In the juxtaposition of horse and woman, the "phallic and ambrosial," McLuhan sees a "chain reaction."[34]

The exact reaction, though, is described in an interesting manner by McLuhan. "Effective advertising," he argues, "gains its ends partly by distracting the attention of the reader from its presuppositions and by its quiet fusion with other levels of experience."[35] By framing *The Mechanical Bride* as an investigation into a broader cultural hypnosis, McLuhan implies that the entire work of advertising—in its language and created experience—is in the Yeatsian mode of trance. This trance is present in pithy advertisements that splash across magazine pages, but it is also cultivated by the "horse opera and soap opera," midcentury entertainment that McLuhan pondered in his final essay in the book. He wondered, "Is it an ideal past specially constructed to justify the ideal future? Or is it just an ideal contrast to a present reality?"[36]

By the time *The Mechanical Bride* was published, its medium almost felt dated. "I failed at that time," McLuhan reflected, "to see that we had already passed out of the mechanistic age into the electronic."[37] McLuhan needed a new subject—an electronic one. By the end of that decade, he would focus on television as the center of his media theory. That medium could "return us to group dynamics, both in theory and in practice" and, in doing so, could cultivate immediate, universal myths.[38]

Although film and television are often thought of together, McLuhan considered them separate in process, purpose, and result. At the time when the pioneers of television were making their 1927 demonstration, films were just starting to experiment with sound. Film was created for a collective audience, to be experienced in a location—a cinema—that often had been repurposed from the medium of theater. Television, though, was homebound, placed in an acoustic space that was designed for living. As early as the late 1950s, McLuhan would argue that television should be understood as light *through*, not light *on*, which separated "television from photography and movie, relating it profoundly to stained glass."[39]

The religious reference was apt. In 1957, Pope Pius XII released *Miranda Prorsus*, his encyclical on motion pictures, radio, and television. These "technical arts," Pius wrote, were more accessible and engaging than "printed books" and "can assuredly provide opportunities for men to meet and unite in common effort." Therefore, the Catholic Church "desires to turn" film, radio, and television "to the extension and furthering of benefits worthy of the name." Of particular interest was television, which Pius—channeling McLuhan's sense—said penetrated the "eye and the ear," offering "events happening far away at the very moment at which they are taking place."[40]

What follows is rather fascinating. Pius assured that such viewing was not passive; rather, the television viewer was "drawn on, as it were, to take an active part" in events—"and this sense of immediacy is increased very much by the home surroundings." Pius affirmed that wholesome programming would need to be created, since the "family circle" would often experience television together, but his pastoral vision is clear: television had unparalleled potential for electronic communion.[41]

Continuing with this trend of the sacred potential for the medium, the next year, Pius named Saint Clare of Assisi as the patron saint of television. In his apostolic letter, Pius explains that the Church must embrace new technology that enables the communication of religious belief. He again references television's unique existence as a medium of home, before sharing the story of Clare, a follower of Saint Francis. One Christmas Eve, Clare was too sick and exhausted to attend Mass at her convent. Although she remained in her room that night, Clare was able to hear the songs of celebration—and saw the image of Christ's manger on her wall. The mystical projection, Pius explained, made Clare the right protector of this medium.[42]

Clare's vision appeared on the wall of a convent, not a screen in the center of a living room, but the correlation is clear: Pius imagined that television could not only make the distant near but place the viewer within the experience. In a letter to the poet Ezra Pound, McLuhan described how "modern machinery" could "[impose] rhythm on human thought and feeling." In the same way that "archaic man" would inhabit the forms of that which he feared—"tiger, bear, wolf—and made it his totem god," modern man sought to get "inside the machine."[43]

Yet McLuhan takes it a step further. Now the machine "is inside us. We in it. Fusion. Oblivion. Safety."[44] As often happens during correspondence, a writer's tone and style near those of his recipient, but beyond McLuhan's syntax remains an observation that would anchor his media theories to come: television works us over, completely. A few weeks after Pius's encyclical, McLuhan was writing to Walter J. Ong, a Jesuit priest and his former student, of media and the Church. The electronic world, McLuhan proclaimed, was of concern to "every catechist and liturgist." In fact, McLuhan thought the "Church has more at stake than anybody. Should set up an institute of Perennial Contemporaryness!"[45]

The Vatican did create such a committee—of which McLuhan was ostensibly a part—but failed to listen to his entreaties to offer concrete contributions. Not one to wait for others, and convinced that his media campaign was part of a broader religious program, McLuhan pressed forward on his own. It was the only way. McLuhan was too idiosyncratic, too performative to be an official representative of his Church, and in being an unofficial one, he was far more influential.

After *The Gutenberg Galaxy* put McLuhan on the media map, interviews, profiles, features, parodies, and explainers followed. Ever the public intellectual, McLuhan played the game well, and in unlikely places. The July 1966 issue of *Vogue* featured Barbara Bach on the cover, shot midtwirl by Richard Avedon, pink, blue, and green paillettes on her dress winking below pink globe earrings by Mimi di Niscemi. Inside, the "People Are Talking About . . ." section featured war, poverty, Jean Genet, Jean-Luc Godard, Vanessa Redgrave, and Marshall McLuhan—a full-page splash of his face with characteristic smirk. "You do something with your mouth and teeth involuntarily when you do something with your eyes," he told the photographer.[46]

Then, across five pages scattered about the issue, McLuhan gets his own space to preach the coming electronic communion. "The American public is about to enter the entertainment industry as participant," he writes. "With the aid of punch cards and computer processing, it is now possible for millions of people to participate directly in programs in prime time." The television audience, through advertising and programming, was now "eligible for custom-made servicing instead of uniform packaging." Yet that audience was itself "an actor in the show."[47]

McLuhan is here to tell us the good word because our environment, that which is our "total surround," tends to create "a condition of non-perception."[48] Most of us don't see; we simply exist. McLuhan—trained in ancient grammar, the Church Fathers, and satirists—could alone see. He was not there to judge; he was there to look. "In TV you are the screen," he told the *Los Angeles Times*, "in movies you are the camera."[49] No matter one's medium, the "business of any performer . . . is to put on the audience, not speak to the audience"—and that included McLuhan himself.[50]

Perhaps McLuhan's greatest put-on was—either ironically or appropriately—one that was largely put on by someone else. His 1967 book *The Medium Is the Massage* arrived in the midst of his mainstream popularity and seemed like the perfect encapsulation of his eccentric theories, random references, and media playfulness. The book is text juxtaposed with image: photograph, diagram, advertising, visual art. The images are often zoomed in, blurred, or cropped. The book is a visual version of the mosaic structure of *The Gutenberg Galaxy*, a sequence of disjointed probes, a rejection of linear narrative. It looks like the work of an artist, and it was.

At this point, McLuhan's brand had been largely shaped by Howard Gossage, an innovative copywriter and advertiser, and Gerald Feigen, a San Francisco doctor who partnered with Gossage to create a consulting firm.[51] Gossage and Feigen introduced McLuhan to magazine editors and writers, including Tom Wolfe, whose *New York* profile led to the widespread mainstream coverage that made McLuhan a pop culture phenomenon. McLuhan caught the attention of Jerome Agel, who the *Village Voice* described as a book producer, one who "writes, edits, designs, lays out, makes up the mechanicals to deliver to the various publishers he contracts with . . . and gets a byline as producer along with collaborators who do the heavy lifting about the subject matter."[52]

In June 1965, Agel wrote to McLuhan and wondered if "a children's book could be developed from *Understanding Media*?"[53] Soon after, McLuhan traveled to New York City to have dinner with Agel and Quentin Fiore, a graphic designer who did work for the Ford Foundation, *Life* magazine, and Bell Laboratories—including designing the numbers on the dial of the standard home phone.[54] The producer and designer were then "anxious" to show McLuhan what they described as "our illustrated mock-up of a book that we are developing based on your published works and per our talk that night at dinner. We don't want to put it into final shape until you have seen and approved our technique."[55]

When the book contract for *The Medium Is the Massage* was announced in March 1966, the marketing capsule noted Fiore's populist design: "Every American comes into contact an average of 10 times a day with one of Mr. Fiore's greatest design achievements: the alphabet that appears on the telephone dial." The book promised to "demonstrate how deeply the new electric technology has restricted man's thoughts, feelings and actions—his *everyday life*, commenting upon some of the consequences of these new perceptions and actions."[56]

McGraw-Hill, McLuhan's publisher, was confused: hadn't he just written a book titled *Understanding Media* about media and its effects? They worried that this new book would be in competition with theirs, but McLuhan assured them, "I didn't write anything for that book. It is excerpts with pictures."[57] The truth is a bit more complicated than

McLuhan's pithy assertion. At each stage of drafting and production, McLuhan examined the manuscript assembled by Fiore and Agel. Fiore explained that there "was no special, 'original' manuscript for the book." Instead, they took McLuhan's work "from previous publications, heavily editing them, and presenting them in isolated 'patches' i.e. individual pages of double-spreads with appropriate accompanying art work, all with a view towards producing a more appealing presentation which would be accessible to a wide public."[58] McLuhan's hand was heaviest during the final proofs, when he made edits and additions.

The Medium Is the Massage had to happen; in a way, it was McLuhan perfected. When it was published in March 1967, Agel proclaimed it to be "the first book designed for the TV age."[59] By early 1968, the book "was already in its eleventh printing and approaching sales of half a million copies."[60] It was a test case for McLuhan's media vision. Detractors thought it was thin on narrative and argument: full of fluff. Yet admirers of McLuhan—even the reluctant ones—couldn't help but admit that McLuhan and his partners had captured what Agel claimed: a book for a generation sustained by home entertainment. "In television," McLuhan affirmed, "images are projected at you. You are the screen. The images wrap around you. You are the vanishing point."[61] The medium, as the title goes, massages us into a sense of relaxation and calm—and we become part of the medium itself.

Forty years after that first television broadcast in Whippany, New Jersey, the medium had truly become the message. Its messenger might seem unlikely, but perhaps that was inevitable. McLuhan himself knew that he was an unusual prophet: "The present is always invisible because it's environmental and saturates the whole field of attention so overwhelmingly; thus everyone but the artist, the man of integral awareness, is alive in an earlier day."[62] McLuhan was an artist of thought: a rhetorical performer whose synthesis of various disciplines was filtered through a religious worldview. In television, McLuhan found a medium that invited the viewer to participate—wholly and, if we are to follow the thought of Pius XII, in a holy way. Even McLuhan's description of television is grounded in transfiguration: "The TV image is a mosaic mesh not only of horizontal lines but of millions of tiny dots, of which the viewer is physiologically able to pick up only 50 or 60 from which he shapes the image; thus he is constantly filling in vague and blurry images, bringing himself into in-depth involvement with the screen and acting out a constant creative dialog with the iconoscope."[63] The viewer's imagination—nearly an act of belief—is essential to completing the image and experience. Television is constantly "tattooing its message directly on our skins," and we are left "an unconscious pointillist painter like Seurat, limning new shapes and images as the iconoscope washes over his entire body."[64] The word—the medium—made flesh. Each of us transfigured in our own homes and yet also connected. McLuhan then had to grapple with perhaps his greatest concern: the spiritual results of a global village.

4

The Global Village

"Oracle? Genius? Carnival Pitchman?" The front page of the *Fordham Ram* wondered if Marshall McLuhan, the school's new $100,000 visiting professor, was worth the money. The Jesuit university in the Bronx bet that McLuhan's short tenure would be both prestigious and provocative. On September 18, 1967, in front of the 178 students enrolled in Communication Arts 141, McLuhan was presented as a sage. Father John Culkin, the Harvard-educated Jesuit who made McLuhan amenable to the masses in an essay about his work that appeared in the *Saturday Review*, said it was "the age of McLuhan." Students cradled copies of his books. The press pined for interviews. The student writer of the article quipped that McLuhan was the "public relations coup of the year."[1]

Embarrassed by the fawning, McLuhan ambled through a twenty-five-minute associative debut lecture about television, attention spans, and how "we do every-thing we can to hide from the present."[2] His mind trav-eled whatever routes it desired, and the audience—captive and captivated—followed. A year earlier, he had offered a pithy explanation of his rhetoric and pedagogy to the *New York Times*: "I don't want them to believe what I say. I just want them to think."[3] He could afford to be evasive. At this point, McLuhan was an international media star with a healthy sense of humor: during his opening lecture, he joked that the most Canadian thing about himself was how he mispronounced *either* and *process*. Afterward, one student concluded, "It was a good show. All the students were perplexed to some extent, but they'll catch on."[4]

Pedagogically, that sounded right. McLuhan said that his teaching would focus on "the training of perception instead of instruction."[5] He would offer probes, nothing more. *The Mechanical Bride* aside, McLuhan was consis-tent on this point: "I have no point of view. I'm a person who swarms over a situation from all aspects simulta-neously. I am a metaphysician of the media. That's why I'm not interested in the moral issues."[6] A moralist would mistake product for process—would miss the environ-ment surrounding the message, which is what McLuhan truly meant when he implored that the medium was the message. There was no time for judgment; observation required all of his focus.

McLuhan's Fordham moment felt rather inevitable: the Catholic-formed media scholar-celebrity, arriving at a Jesuit institution in New York City, the media capital of the world, with the freedom to develop lectures, film presen-tations, and mentor independent study work for students who didn't always understand him—but understood that he was worth their attention.

McLuhan's paradoxes were on full display at the university. He could be hip and dated. He could make eerily sharp points and follow his syntactic mazes to jokes with muted punchlines. He could understand the world of his students better than them. That world was shaped by television. As McLuhan noted in his first lecture, television created a huge emotional and social gap between parents and children, children and teachers. Television viewers, McLuhan argued, sought depth in the form of multimodal experience and immersion—which demonstrates for McLuhan a sense of engagement.[7]

The medium of television could deliver this engagement. Its function was to envelop us. "As an entirely electric medium," McLuhan would later write, "TV also has much greater power [than film] to 'transport' us and to transform our awareness. There is, as it were, an 'angelic' dimension in electric media, lacking even to the movie."[8] We are transported, and apparently transfigured, by this electric continuum. Whatever McLuhan's misgivings about the content of this medium, its structure and possibilities were clear: "The new electronic interdependence recreates the world in the image of a global village."[9]

The global village was immediate, absolute, and communal. It was glorious with possibility—and at the same time dangerous. McLuhan began consistently using the term *global village* around 1959 and considered it the conclusion of the print book's evolution as a medium. The book was a solitary experience—even though many could be reading the same book, the individual's experience

with the book is private. The global village of the telephone, the television, and what would become the digital
world of the internet results in a change in not only the
content we receive but the way we think. A self-admitted
traditionalist, McLuhan played with sixties-era speak:
with it meant to be in the know, aware, cool. But for
McLuhan, it also meant to be attached and connected,
always with something potentially powerful and imper-
sonal. The transformation from print to electronic media
meant a movement from message to vessel—the world
becomes small and immediate. The "tribal" coming of the
world predicted the world of social media, a development
of particular concern to a writer for whom communion is
not mere metaphor.

When McLuhan spoke to those Fordham students,
he was inhabiting what he called "Acoustic Space": a
"spherical" location that is "without bounds or vanishing points." In its infinity, it is not a "container," nor is
it "hollowed out": its structure is defined by "pitch separation and kinesthesia." Previously, only writing codified
"the acoustic into the visual."[10] Television could do that
and much more. In a May 1959 letter, McLuhan posited
that the "Electronic Age"—with its mode of reproduction
and patterning through "instantaneous flow of information from every part of a situation, from every quarter"—
fundamentally changed our conceptions of space and time.
In this new world, "whatever happens to anybody, happens
to everybody."[11]

It is worth acknowledging that as early as 1960—more
than sixty years before I type these words—McLuhan
predicted "When the globe becomes a single electronic

computer, with all its languages and cultures recorded on the single tribal drum, the fixed point of view of print culture becomes irrelevant and impossible, no matter how precious."[12] In such an electronic world, "any marginal area can become center, and marginal experiences can be had at any center."[13]

Critics of McLuhan have cataloged the moments when his predictions missed or when his rhetoric smothered his reason. His aphoristic observations could sometimes sound trite, especially when examined through our contemporary mode of cynicism. The internet is often a profoundly pessimistic place: a repository for conspiracy theories that have developed into metanarratives, a place where anonymous avatars troll and tussle with abandon. In many ways, the space of the internet cultivates and rewards skepticism—which means a literature professor turned media theorist was a most unlikely prophet.

This was McLuhan's power, in a sense: he was not supposed to have figured all of this out. In January 1966, McLuhan told Tom Wolfe that in every "organization, each individual tends to have a point of view. The consultant who is called in to diagnose has the advantage of not having a point of view."[14] We might consider McLuhan a cultural consultant. He was outdated and outmoded during his own time, his identity a dramatization of tension between that which is obsolete and obsolescent. Yet now he fits perfectly into our digital present; McLuhan's mosaic method of disjointed interpretation matches our harried lives. McLuhan's time wasn't ready for him. We are.

"The global village" has become one of McLuhan's core taglines, and its ad-speak simplicity makes it seem almost superficial. Yet McLuhan returned to the phrase again and again, evolving and expanding and sometimes even undermining it at points in his books, lectures, interviews, and television appearances. Perhaps even more so than "the medium is the message," "the global village" was a lifetime slogan turned project. Though the term may seem shallow, tracking his usage and modification of it reveals how his observation holds a spiritual resonance.

In 1959, the National Association of Educational Broadcasters commissioned McLuhan to research and write the Understanding Media Project, the goal of which was to "develop materials and the basis for instruction in the meanings and uses of the new media of TV and radio (in the context of other media) in American elementary and secondary schools."[15] In the months prior, McLuhan had been corresponding with Harry J. Skornia, the association president, about such a project, with the McLuhan-suggested title *Understanding Media*. In one letter, McLuhan ponders angles for the project that might best secure government funding. He argues that "for centuries educators have lived under the monarchy of printing," but with the newer media of "photography, movie, telegraph, telephone, radio, and television," educators "now face students who, in terms of the information-flow of their experience, spend all their waking hours in classrooms without walls, as it were."[16]

Later in that December 1958 letter, McLuhan reiterates that "students are faced with a phalanx of technologies which convey great quantities of information with global range and content."[17] From McLuhan's perspective, if teachers could be converted to thinking with and through the new media, then the populist results could be significant. McLuhan's project was not geared toward undergraduates or doctoral students; his aim was to modify the way that high school students were instructed. High school was the great populist education experiment, where the mass users and consumers of the media resided.

"Obsession with 'content' seems infallibly to obscure the structural changes effected by media," McLuhan wrote in the summary of his project aims.[18] Roughly a year later, in his completed report, McLuhan formulated the idea as one of his operating assumptions: "that the absence of [understanding of media effects] was eloquent testimony to the power of media to anesthetize those very modes of awareness in which they were most operative."[19]

McLuhan was not the first, and certainly not the last, to propose radical changes to secondary school pedagogy without practical consideration of daily life in the class-room. His final report was too ahead of its time—and yet, like so much of his oeuvre, perfect for the digital age. "Even our visual experience is now a mosaic of items assembled from every part of the globe, moment by moment," McLuhan wrote. "Lineal perspective and pictorial organization can-not cope with this situation."[20]

The concept of the global village was now becoming an anchor and referent for McLuhan, as in a 1961 book review titled "The Electric Culture." "The collective night world of the tribe will undergo the same illumination that our social lives have done via electricity," McLuhan wrote. "Likewise the electric movement of information abolishes the walls and boundaries between subject matters as much as between night and day and nationalities. The tribalism will consist of one tribe in one global village—to wit, the human family."[21]

The point returned the next year in *The Gutenberg Galaxy.* Early in the book, he affirms a nearly spiritual union created through worldwide communication: "Our extended faculties and senses now constitute a single field of experience which demands that they become collectively conscious."[22] New technology creates shock and disorder. Then there is the response: the "adjustment" to this new technology, where daily personal and public life conforms to the shift. The global village was "quickly recreating in us the mental processes of the most primitive men."[23] As Walter J. Ong, SJ, wrote, McLuhan's conception of a global consciousness in the book was patently true, even among those who "who do not even think of the sensorium as such under that name."[24]

The following year, in a short essay titled "The Agenbite of Outwit," McLuhan began cultivating a theory that "electronic media are . . . extensions of the central nervous system, an inclusive and simultaneous field." Whether we are watching television or even driving a car, our participation in the mechanical-electronic world conforms to the structure and requirements of that world—so that "we become servo-mechanisms of our contrivances, responding to them in the immediate, mechanical way that they demand of us." The new Narcissus myth was not a love of our own image but our tendency to "fall in love with extensions of themselves which [people] are convinced are not extensions of themselves."[25]

All of us, in love with our extended selves, participate in "a kind of orchestral, resonating unity, not the unity of logical discourse." McLuhan cautioned that the result is unsettling, "a total uneasiness, as of a man wearing his skull inside and his brain outside. We have become peculiarly vulnerable."[26]

In 1964's *Understanding Media*—the final, evolved manuscript of his earlier education project—McLuhan would again rely on the global village as an anchoring concept. "Contracted" by electronics, McLuhan wrote, "action and the reaction occur almost at the same time."[27] McLuhan went even further than this contraction; the electronic transfiguration results in humans "being translated more and more into the form of information, moving toward the technological extension of consciousness."[28]

As McLuhan follows this reasoning in *Understanding Media*, he employs religious vocabulary to encapsulate the changes. This translation is one of bodies to a "spiritual form of information."[29] The most perfect medium for this translation is the computer, which promises "a means of instant translation of any code or language into any other code or language. The computer, in short, promises by technology a Pentecostal condition of universal understanding and unity."[30] That McLuhan would use such religious language and references in private, and in his letters, is not surprising; that he would use them in public reveals that the spiritual foundation to his media theories was laid bare.

For some reason, this spiritual foundation has been referenced by biographers in relative passing; it has never quite been ignored, but it also has not been illuminated. In his books, lectures, and television appearances, McLuhan consistently employed not only religious language and references but a religious sensibility: the Catholic and particularly

Jesuit-influenced view that God exists in all things. Rather than a biographical footnote, this recognition enables us to wed McLuhan's disparate interests and ideas into a cohesive thesis—and makes the complaints of detractors appear narrow in comparison to the holistic nature of his vision.

In a 1965 BBC interview with the literary critic Frank Kermode, McLuhan explained that our shift from the mechanical to electrical world has resulted "in an enormous increase in the amount of information that is moving." In a world where information swirls around us, the only way to survive is through "pattern recognition"—something akin to the tendency of imagist poets to parse the world into finite images linked by themes. We are not merely observers of these patterns—we participate within them: "Everything under electric conditions is looped. You become folded over into yourself. Your image of yourself changes completely."[31]

None of this happens in a personal or cultural vacuum, for the mediums through which we engage in these looping patterns—television and now the internet—are reproduced across the world. McLuhan certainly did not think this electronic communion was always, or even often, seamless. As he noted in *Vogue* in 1966, our "electronic world of all-at-onceness" means that "things hit into each other but in which there are no connections." This immediacy is in contrast to the print world, when the public was "a large group of separate individuals accessible through a common language and a common national territory." The public of the electric world is more engaged and more involved with one another and with a common set of texts and events—including "trivial events," which, "when circulated at electric speeds, can acquire enormous potential and influence."[32] Such triviality takes a toll on our spirits. In electric media, as our experiences "begin to include everybody else, many people are inclined to feel that they have lost their private identity altogether. Instead of feeling enriched, they feel deprived."[33]

The global village could be disastrous or wonderful—or both. Two different interviews from 1969 demonstrate the duality of McLuhan's thinking. In a conversation with Gerald E. Stearn, who edited an anthology of reactions to McLuhan and offered him the last word via an interview, McLuhan was pessimistic. "It never occurred to me that uniformity and tranquility were the properties of the global village," McLuhan affirmed. "It has more spite and envy." As if there could be any misunderstanding, McLuhan said, "I don't *approve* of the global village. I say we live in it."[34] In this global, claustrophobic village, there occurs a violent massage: "the shaping, the twisting, the bending of the whole human environment by the technology."[35] Humanity sounds more wounded than enlightened.

Yet another interview that year with *Playboy* took a more optimistic approach. While his biographer Philip Marchand wondered whether McLuhan was playing to his audience, that suggestion implies that there was any public McLuhan other than one grounded in performance. In a wide-ranging interview, McLuhan argued that the electronic world results in "an amplification of human consciousness on a world scale" and would soon be supplanted by the computer's "integral cosmic unconsciousness." Unlike the sniveling realm of the global village, McLuhan also wondered if the computer "holds out the promise of a technologically engendered state of universal understanding and unity, a state of absorption in the logos that could knit mankind into one family and create a perpetuity of collective harmony and peace." Although McLuhan used catchphrases like "psychic communal integration" in the interview, his true goal was more ecumenical than esoteric: "In a Christian sense, this is merely a new interpretation of the mystical body of Christ; and Christ, after all, is the ultimate extension of man."[36]

The difference between the universal consciousness of freeform, psychedelic narrative and the unified body of the world in Christian theology is Christ—and McLuhan's deep belief suggests that his meanderings into the language of his time were not merely a skilled rhetorician following the routes of his audience. He hated the possibility of gossip and triviality that pervaded the global village, and he wasn't fond of the recent liturgical transformations to Mass, but his Catholic faith implored him to recognize God in all things. In the words of Father Culkin, McLuhan's hesitancy to judge while making media observations was "very much in keeping with the Pauline view of charity."[37]

In a 1977 appearance on *The Mike McManus Show*, McLuhan sounded like Timothy Leary turned monk: "Everybody has become porous. The light and the message go right through us. At this moment, we are on the air. We do not have any physical body. When you're on the telephone or on radio or on T.V., you don't have a physical body—you're just an image on the air. When you don't have a physical body, you're a discarnate being. You have a very different relation to the world around you. I think this has been one of the big effects of the electric age. It has deprived people really of their identity."[38] No longer individuals, we are one.

The *global* element of the "global village" is therefore obvious: McLuhan knew the electric, instant world would evolve beyond national borders. His choice of *village* also seems appropriate—a regional space where oral culture thrives—but McLuhan might have chosen a *city* or *suburb* (that he did not reveals his penchant for probes as advertising slogans—"global village" is nearly alliterative, paradoxically nostalgic). His Catholic contemporary and self-admitted admirer, the novelist Thomas Pynchon, pondered the metaphorical possibilities of suburban layout in his 1967 novel *The Crying of Lot 49*.

Early in the novel, Oedipa Maas, a suburban housewife who becomes the executrix for her rich, mysterious exboyfriend's will, is driving from Kinneret to San Narciso, where he lived. Upon driving there on a Sunday morning, she "looked down a slope, needing to squint for the sunlight, onto a vast sprawl of houses which had grown up all together, like a well-tended crop, from the dull brown earth." That ecological simile is soon replaced by an electronic metaphor: "She thought of the time she'd opened a transistor radio to replace a battery and seen her first printed circuit. The ordered swirl of houses and streets, from this high angle, sprang at her now with the same unexpected, astonishing clarity as the circuit card had." Although "she knew even less about radios than about Southern Californians," she concludes that "there were to both outward patterns a hieroglyphic sense of concealed meaning, of an intent to communicate."[39]

On that Sunday morning, surrounded by thick smog and blanched by the sunlight, she felt "at the centre of an odd, religious instant."[40] A reader of McLuhan, Pynchon shows an affinity for imagining how our physical surroundings contain or elicit modes of communication—and perhaps communication is the lens through which we should best understand the global village. We cannot possibly have a connection without some method of communication.

A focus on communication helps reveal the spiritual possibilities of the global village. After Father Culkin introduced McLuhan to the mainstream reading masses, he revised his essay for a more religious audience. In "A Churchman's Guide to Marshall McLuhan," Culkin writes toward the *Religious Education* interfaith readership of ministers, priests, preachers, and other clergy involved in education and public dialogue. He notes that communication is endemic to McLuhan's project: "His works demand a high degree of participation and involvement from the reader. They are poetic and intuitive rather than logical and analytic."[41]

Culkin proves to be one of McLuhan's best translators, and evangelists, for this religious audience. Channeling his colleague's theories, Culkin opines that it is "interesting to note that the Reformation which broke up Christianity rode the fragmenting medium of print and that Ecumenism is riding the electronic surf of radio and television." The electronic return to orality, Culkin argues, is a return to Biblical originality and context: "The literal approach to scripture came with the Gutenberg era and departs with the electronic age."[42]

Culkin then explicitly frames McLuhan's media theories, including the global village, as patently religious in nature and function: "McLuhan maintains that the electronic environment has provided many of the unifying elements proper to the concept of the people of God as Christ's body. . . . On a technological level the world is almost literally becoming one body laced with an intricate electronic nervous system."[43]

Culkin concludes his essay with fascinating questions in the tradition of McLuhan: "Does it make any sense to line up the following three words—communication, community, communion? Can the scriptures be reinterpreted in communication terms? Can the Trinity serve as a communications model?"[44]

These were questions that the Catholic Church wanted—needed—to answer. On December 4, 1963, during the Second Vatican Council, the "Decree on the Means of Social Communication" affirmed that a "special office of the Holy See is at the disposal of the Sovereign Pontiff in the exercise of his supreme pastoral responsibility for the means of social communication."[45] In January 1971, that office, which had taken the name of the Pontifical Council for Social Communications, released pastoral instructions that sounded McLuhanesque.

"The media of social communication can contribute a great deal to human unity," the decree stipulated, but "if good will is not there, this outpouring of technology may produce an opposite effect so that there is less understanding and more discord and, as a result, evils are multiplied."[46] Communication, at its most profound moments, "is the giving of self in love."[47] Radio and television were "bonds of union for those who cannot share physically in the life of the Church because of their sickness or old age"[48] and also were especially useful in connecting with those "who have no affiliation with any Church and yet subconsciously seek spiritual nourishment." The conclusion was simple: "The Church cannot afford to ignore such opportunities."[49]

Had the Catholic Church listened to McLuhan? The truth is complicated. As early as *Understanding Media*, McLuhan alluded to the Church's awareness of communication, noting that "Pope Pius XII was deeply concerned that there be serious study of the media" as early as 1950.[50] Jesuits read, quoted, and spoke of McLuhan widely. Pope John XXIII named McLuhan to a related committee; although McLuhan's expertise was not directly solicited in any discussion, research, or creation of documents, his influence on their central ideas and language was clear.[51]

This was more than mere coincidence. One of McLuhan's gifts was his ability to understand how faith and media, as forms of communication, would inevitably intersect. Derrick de Kerckhove, one of McLuhan's Toronto colleagues, said that "McLuhan's faith was a seamless totality which informed and shaped his thoughts and his life." When de Kerckhove asked McLuhan directly what faith meant to him, McLuhan answered, "Paying attention, faith is paying attention, not to the cliches of religion only, but to the ground of the total man, which is the archetype. You come to the faith by prayer and by paying attention."[52]

For McLuhan, there was not a separate faith that was then cultivated into a media theory. His entire way of seeing was framed through his religious belief. There was no need for McLuhan to regularly affirm his Catholicism in public in the same way that we do not meter out our heartbeats—his belief was habitual, entire, absolute. The medium or environment of the global village was inevitable for McLuhan, for the entire world existed from Christ. The fact that McLuhan knew the global village would also breed strife does not neuter this truth; instead, it suggests the importance of faith to combat such dissension.

Walter J. Ong, SJ, notes that Christ was "both mediator and message," as demonstrated in John 1:14: "The Word was made flesh and dwelt among us." Following Aquinas, Ong—whose analysis of orality both overlapped with McLuhan's and extended his former teacher's theories—notes that Christ "knew reading and writing, as the Gospels clearly report, but conveyed what he had to say not by his own writing but by preaching and personal association, leaving behind him not a corpus of books he had written but an oral tradition in a community." Ong reminds us, "*He* is what he *means*."[53] Elsewhere, Ong writes that in the Christian vision, "the Word is here the proper name of a Person, the Son of God, himself God—*eo verbum quo filius*. . . . 'He is Word by the fact that he is Son.'"[54] In the person and presence of Christ, Ong and McLuhan see a spiritual precedent for the global village—the communion of all.

"In the old hardware world," McLuhan wrote, "all roads led to Rome." In the age of the global village, "there are no roads. Rome is in our sitting room as much as Vietnam." The reforms of the Second Vatican Council had decentralized the Church so that "new participation of the faithful in the decision-making process exceeds even the fragmentation of Protestant literacy."[55] The global village, via "the electric circuit," has "restored us to the world of pattern recognition and to an understanding of life of forms which had been denied to all but the artists of the now receding mechanical age."[56]

"The global village" ultimately became as much of a tagline for McLuhan as his iconic "The medium is the message." In 1967, George Gent wrote for the *New York Times*, "Television's unique capability of turning the world into 'a global village,' to use Marshall McLuhan's perceptive phrase, was demonstrated yesterday with its magnificent coverage of Pope Paul VI's visit to the Roman Catholic shrine of Our Lady of Fatima in Portugal."[57] Over one hundred million viewers worldwide—including nearly half of all television viewers in New York City—watched the pope's pilgrimage. A few months later, McLuhan would arrive at Fordham to much fanfare, where his media theories could be anchored in the communication capital of the world.

Life had other plans.

After the initial hype, the undergraduates—a notoriously skeptical bunch—responded to McLuhan's lectures with a "depressing chorus of stares, stirrings and coughs," a reporter noted.[58] In turn, McLuhan could be short with them. What began as occasional blackouts became more frequent, sometimes occurring during classes—resulting in Father Culkin taking over some lectures, to the confused looks of students. A few months into his visiting term at Fordham, McLuhan was out of the classroom and at Columbia Presbyterian Hospital—anxiously awaiting surgery to have a brain tumor removed. McLuhan's surgery was notable not only for its celebrity patient; the procedure "had been the longest neurosurgical operation in the history of American medicine."[59] He remained in the hospital until December 12. He returned to teach in the spring semester, but his recovery dampened. The surgery—and the big city—had taken a toll on him. A *Harper's* feature from 1965 now sounded prophetic: McLuhan "treasures his life in Toronto precisely because it is well away from the great communications and fashion centers; he sees them better, he thinks, from the perspective of distance."[60] Now the sage was in the middle of the village and longed to escape.

In January 1968, McLuhan was working in his small campus office when Culkin stopped by with William Kuhns, the previous visiting lecturer. "Marshall's face sagged and he was still pale," Kuhns recalled, from the continuing recovery. McLuhan was using a pencil to write his speech, but it had snapped. Kuhns offered him a ballpoint pen. "It'll change what I'm writing, you know," McLuhan joked.[61]

Tired, but still clever, McLuhan finished the term. In September, McLuhan returned home to Saint Michael's in Toronto for the fall semester, leaving his Fordham residency a confounding jumble of possibilities. The University of Toronto's president Claude Bissell and his wife, Christine, threw a lavish and lively welcoming party at their residence. Well-dressed guests talked, joked, laughed, ate, and drank while a slideshow of McLuhan photographs was projected onto a screen. All of the guests pinned a button to their suits and dresses—emblazoned with the face of the guest of honor and a slogan: "God Bless You Marshall McLuhan."

5

A Digital Patron Saint

On October 19, 1969, an SDS Sigma 7 in Boelter Hall at the University of California, Los Angeles, logged on to an SDS 940 at the Stanford Research Institute. We might say that the two computers communicated—but the mode of communication was nothing like an email or text. UCLA typed a letter, and Stanford received it. First an *L*, then an *O*, and then a *G*—which caused the SDS 940 at Stanford to crash. Taken liberally and poetically, then, the first abbreviated communication between two host computers was a religiously infused term: *Lo.*[1]

Marshall McLuhan, one might assume, would have described such an occurrence as both a sign and a wonder. A few months earlier, in an expansive interview with *Playboy*, McLuhan had pondered the possibilities of computers. Computers might enable us to ditch traditional languages for "an integral cosmic unconsciousness" in the mode of

Henri Bergson's collective biological memory.[2] Computers, McLuhan opined, were not meant to mine or even transmit information; they were meant to transform our environments.

Luddites, McLuhan warned, should get ready to be disappointed. There would be no Ned Ludd marauding in the night to "smash all machinery to bits, so we might as well sit back and see what is happening and what will happen to us in a cybernetic world."[3] Better yet, we might embrace what is coming—the arrival for McLuhan of nothing less than a transformation: "The new man, linked in a cosmic harmony that transcends time and space, will sensuously caress and mold and pattern every facet of the terrestrial artifact as if it were a work of art, and man himself will become an organic art form." McLuhan lamented that his own inevitable passing would leave much of the coming progress "tantalizingly unread," and yet, "the story begins only when the book closes."[4]

If we think that McLuhan is being unduly or uncharacteristically poetic here, we are ignoring nearly two decades of his pronouncements. McLuhan thought the world—or even more so, the future—belonged to the vision of artists, and he hoped to participate in the divination. Although not a creative writer, McLuhan was undoubtedly a creative thinker. Critics note that his works lack footnotes and citations, implying that his scholarship was shoddy. Perhaps McLuhan's status as a professor compelled people to read him as a product of the academy, but he claimed to be the opposite. Why would one who sought to transform education from the secondary to graduate levels remain bound to tradition? McLuhan read widely and deeply. He had the scholarly capacity to exist in the established academic tradition, but his project had other concerns.

His genre has been misread. He was not a traditional scholar. McLuhan was a prose-poet, a writer of almost mystical visions. He was a rhetorician, a performer, and perhaps a priest of sorts. McLuhan was a poet of the media, an artist who realized that an extemporaneous mode of communication worked better to capture the realities of his changing world than traditional literary techniques.

In a March 1964 letter, McLuhan describes his fascination with one of Andy Warhol's pop art shows. His fellow Catholic artist "uses the technique of redundancy and repetition to transform the pictorial into the iconic."[5] McLuhan's method of mosaic writing—characterized by vignettes, association, fragmentation, and a homiletic tendency to make grand pronouncements—feels downright Warholian. Yet McLuhan's prose was not influenced by Warhol, and neither was the iconic artist formed by the media theorist. Their Catholicism—filtered through artistic modes that ranged from the profound to the profane—resulted in a vision of the world in which disparate images, experiences, and ideas were all unified by God. McLuhan and Warhol might have both wished that the world embraced Christ. They were both believing Christians. Yet more importantly, they recognized that a religious vision of the world offered the most flexible and persuasive metaphors.

Unfortunately, cultures often pillory their prophets, and McLuhan was no different. After a decade of wild popularity, his media reign came to an end. On December 26, 1969, legendary *Los Angeles Times* columnist Jack

Smith made his judgment: "Of all the odd saints and gurus the decade delivered us, perhaps the strangest was Marshall McLuhan. He is thought of vaguely as a seer, the high priest of the Age of Communications. He was really the Andy Warhol of academe. He walked about ringing his cracked bell to toll, prematurely, the death of the written word. He set out in his little paper boat to subdue the mighty sea of language, and was drowned."[6]

Columns are dashed for deadlines, and bombast is the mode—but Smith's invective captures a trend of McLuhan's glib detractors. They thought McLuhan was a fraud, a performer. They perhaps vaguely intoned his spiritual sensibility but did so more to mock his perceived prophecies than to engage his religious belief. They mistook his view of coming obsolescence for the claim that something was obsolete. This misunderstood him; they parodied him.

Many criticisms of McLuhan were misrepresentations of things about his personality that we might celebrate. "Probes, to be effective, must have this edge, strength, pressure. Of course they *sound* very dogmatic," McLuhan said in an interview. "That doesn't mean you are committed to them. You may toss them away."[7] McLuhan *was* putting on a show, just like his mother, the elocutionist. Just like James Joyce.

Yet Smith's framing was at least prescient of the coming critical response. If the sixties belonged to McLuhan, the seventies belonged to berating him. First up, and most infamous, was Jonathan Miller, a British physician turned actor and director. Miller, a deft writer, wielded his knives at McLuhan in a 1971 profile book. He deserves credit for being one of the first critics to consider McLuhan's

Catholicism—but does so for polemical reasons. Early in the book, Miller ties McLuhan to Teilhard de Chardin, who was certainly an influence on McLuhan from as early as *The Gutenberg Galaxy*. But Miller wasn't interested in understanding how a Jesuit paleontologist might have offered a Canadian media scholar some esoteric metaphors.

"Like de Chardin," Miller notes, "McLuhan is a Catholic, and although he makes no specific reference to the fact, it adds a hidden bias to all his famous opinions and thus makes nonsense of his claim to have freed himself from the tyranny of 'values.' As I hope to show later, the bulk of McLuhan's work is strongly animated by Catholic piety and the bid for detachment is partly a tactical stance designed to deceive 'the enemy.'"[8] The jab reeks of the old antipapist sentiment that Rome controls Catholics. Miller never delivers on his attempt to reveal the contours of McLuhan's Catholic foundation and influence—but that assumes such inquiry was his intention. Still, McLuhan was, in many ways, an easy target: a man of religion who made grand proclamations.

Criticism of McLuhan was warranted, necessary, and inevitable—the theorist prodded and provoked. Yet criticism is often clothed in ideology and bias, and when McLuhan's detractors got a whiff of his papist allegiance, they went after him. McLuhan, they thought, had been up to something all along. This was true, of course, but not exactly in the way they claimed. At the height of his media visibility, McLuhan told the *Los Angeles Times* that the "business of any performer . . . is to put on the audience, not speak to the audience."[9] Put on, prod, provoke. McLuhan was fulfilling the role of a showman.

"At 4 a.m. Herbert Marshall McLuhan, hip prophet of the '60s," so goes a 1976 profile in *People*, "awakens in his Toronto bedroom and slips into an ancient green bathrobe. He hurries into the kitchen not for breakfast but for a taste of biblical scholarship. For an hour he pores over scriptures in Greek, Latin, French, German and English, while gnawing on an orange." This version of McLuhan was gently mainstream: an eccentric homebody who eats breakfast in "Hawaiian shirt and slacks" and who likes to rest: "Second only to his devout faith in Catholicism is his belief in the catnap."[10]

Between the time of Miller's takedown and the *People* feature, McLuhan had receded from the front pages of magazines. He still published books, but they were often partnerships with other writers. He still gave speeches. He still made probes. Yet he had slowed down, weathered from recurring health problems.

That didn't stop people from calling on McLuhan; he had, perhaps, graduated from the regular main event to distant legend. In one morning, his secretary fielded inquiries from Woody Allen (for McLuhan's upcoming cameo in *Annie Hall*), the governor of California, Radio Québec, BBC, Denver-based computer executives, and the representatives for the Smothers Brothers. Nuns and priests were almost daily visitors to his home around lunch and were often served McLuhan's eccentric specialty: a mixture of "two different cans of Campbell's soup." Meanwhile, McLuhan continued to affirm his fundamental role as a seeker: "Once you decide to become an explorer, there's no place to stop."[11]

Best known for his ability to diagnose the evolving present, McLuhan turned his eye toward the future. In one of his last publications, a series of predictions for *Maclean's* magazine written in 1979, McLuhan looked toward the next decade. "In the '80s," McLuhan wrote, "there will be a general awareness that the technology game is out of control, and that perhaps man was not intended to live at the speed of light." He predicted "a dramatic increase in the conservative backlash against runaway technology and change." Rapid and rampant change would breed isolation. Forced to continually adapt to new environments, people would feel further strained from their communities. Collectively, communities would resemble "an anemic individual without the energy to adapt to the demands of survival."[12]

McLuhan's predictions were grim. When our lives are dictated by the speed of electronic light, we will become merely "an item in the data bank—software only, easily forgotten—and deeply resentful." We will lose our bodies and be "transformed into abstract information which is electric software," causing us to potentially lose "all relation to natural law or human responsibility or moral obligation." In such a technologically saturated world, our only salvation will come from turning inward: "an extreme example of hardware shifting to software and to spiritual values."[13]

McLuhan spent the final days of the first year of the eighties with Frank Stroud, a Jesuit priest. They originally met in 1974 but had been out of touch until mid-December 1980, when Stroud was invited by John Culkin—who by then had left the priesthood to pursue his media advocacy—to a film seminar in New York City. Also present was McLuhan's daughter Teri, a filmmaker who had told Stroud that he should "visit her father."[14] Stroud originally was going to wait until the semester break in January. Instead, he went in late December. He would be McLuhan's final visitor.

Stroud would later note that "God literally lifted me up from Jersey City and planted me down in Wychwood Park Toronto to complete the Jesuit connection." Stroud said Mass at the McLuhan home, and "from that moment on Marshall seemed not to want me to leave his side." They walked together around Wychwood Park. They talked about the many letters and miscellany that McLuhan received, including a cartoon sketched by Tom Wolfe.[15] McLuhan, in poor health, listened as Stroud read him selections from articles and books. The last book McLuhan read in his life—or rather listened to—was *Ignatius of Loyola* by Karl Rahner, SJ, an illustrated biography of the Jesuit founder.[16]

Then, on December 30, Stroud again celebrated Mass—this time "using a bottle of fine Burgundy a colleague of McLuhan's had brought back from France."[17] McLuhan and the priest had cigars and then went down to the basement, where McLuhan kept his television. He'd moved the set there a few years earlier: "I did not want it invading my home."[18] McLuhan told his daughter that he didn't want to go to bed yet. He and the Jesuit watched the eleven o'clock news. When the news broadcast ended, they went back upstairs. Before he left, Stroud and McLuhan hugged. McLuhan finally went to bed.[19] He was found dead the next morning.

A lover of hymns, perhaps McLuhan had gone to bed humming his favorite selection, "Mine Eyes Have Seen the Glory of the Coming of the Lord." Hours earlier, Stroud, during his final Mass at the McLuhan home, had intoned the *nunc dimittis*—the Song of Simeon. The priest had lifted his hands as if he was holding the Christ child and said, "Lord, now you are letting your servant depart in peace, according to your word."[20] Simeon, now that he had seen the Savior of the World, could die.

* * *

In *Videodrome* (1983), a film by acclaimed director David Cronenberg, Max Renn is president of Toronto's Civic TV, "the one you take to bed with you." He's always looking for the next provocation to broadcast: sex, violence, and mayhem are all welcomed. Screen shock is victimless, he claims, saying "I give my viewers a harmless outlet for their fantasies and their frustrations." But Max wants more for his meager Channel 83. He's "looking for something that will break through." He finds the ultimate shock in the form of a pirated video: a dramatized snuff film called *Videodrome*, shot in a small red room, with black-garbed torturers and their female victims.

The film is an homage to all things small screen: local access, low budget, low resolution. Max, played by a smirking James Woods, will do anything to titillate his viewers, but he's a sneaky moralist. "Better on TV than on the streets," he says of violence. Max thinks that he's controversial, but he soon learns that other provocateurs have what he lacks: a philosophy.

In response to criticism of his network's programming, Max appears on a television talk show along with Brian O'Blivion, who is described as a "media prophet professor."

Unlike the other panel members, he appears via television screen. His gray hair is receding. He has a mustache and looks much more formal than the other guests. Dressed in a suit and a tie, he appears more like a professor of literature than a vanguard media theorist. "The television screen has become the retina of the mind's eye," O'Blivion says. "That's why I refuse to appear on television, except *on* television. Of course O'Blivion isn't the name I was born with, it's my television name. Soon all of us will have special names. Names designed to cause the cathode ray tube to resonate." Those recursive lines, peppered with vagaries and paradoxes that sound innately truthful, are familiar in sound and sense.

In his audio commentary for the film, Cronenberg admits that the professor was inspired by the "communications guru" Marshall McLuhan. McLuhan taught at the University of Toronto while Cronenberg attended the college, but to his "everlasting regret," the director never took a course with the media icon. Cronenberg said that McLuhan's "influence was felt everywhere at the university" —a mystical-tinged description that McLuhan would have appreciated. "I did read everything he wrote," Cronenberg said of McLuhan.[21]

During his appearance on the talk show, Max flirts with another guest, Nicki Brand (played by Debbie Harry), radio host of *The Emotional Rescue Show*. They go back to his apartment, and he jokingly asks if she wants to watch *Videodrome*. He's taken aback when Nicki likes the disturbing film and further unsettled when he sees gashes on her neck. Max prefers fantasy, but Nicki's flesh has been wounded. When she later jokes that she's going to audition for *Videodrome* herself, Max pleads for her to stay away from those "mondo video weirdo guys."

Max soon learns from an agent who secures programming for the station that *Videodrome* is an actual snuff film. Partially because he wants the show for Civic TV—but mostly because he fears for Nicki's safety—Max tries to track down the video's origins. The trail leads Max to the Cathode Ray Mission, its red and blue sign complemented with the Sacred Heart. A crowd of homeless people sifts into the building, where they kneel in front of televisions. They suffer from the disease of electronic disconnection: "Watching TV will help patch them back into the world's mixing-board." The scene feels like a dystopian Catholic vision of the detritus of the global village.

Max is there to find O'Blivion, but the mysterious professor is absent. "I am my father's screen," his daughter Bianca says. She recognizes Max from the show, quipping, "you said some very superficial things: violence, sex, imagination, catharsis."

I am my father's screen—more than an errant line of dialogue. Cronenberg, among other artists, thinkers, and theorists, would become McLuhan's screen for later generations. They did not merely continue his memory; they resurrected his vision. They proved him right.

Max later receives a video cassette recording of O'Blivion, who predicts that the "battle for the mind of North America will be fought in the video arena," because "the screen is part of the physical structure of the brain. Therefore, whatever appears on the television screen emerges as raw experience for those who watch it. Therefore, television is reality and reality is less than television." Then O'Blivion begins to talk to Max directly through the video, saying that he had a "brain tumor" that caused visions. "I believe the visions caused the tumor, and not the reverse"—a rather base acknowledgment that McLuhan's experimental perception of the world was accompanied by neurological issues.

Max can't keep cool. He is infected by *Videodrome*; the show's reality subverts its unreal medium. Max discovers that Professor O'Blivion—the perversion of McLuhan—helped create *Videodrome* because "he saw it as the next phase in the evolution of man as a technological animal." Sustained viewing of *Videodrome* creates tumors and hallucinations. Max is being tricked by the remaining originators of *Videodrome*, who proclaim, "North America's getting soft, and the rest of the world is getting tough. We're entering savage new times, and we're going to have to be pure and direct and strong if we're going to survive them." *Videodrome* is a way to identify the derelicts by giving them what they most crave—real violence—and then incapacitate them into submission.

McLuhan's idea that "mental breakdown is the very common result of uprooting and inundation with new information" and his simultaneous interest in, and skepticism of, the "electric eye" finds a gory literalism in Cronenberg's film. *Videodrome* is what happens when a self-described existentialist-atheist channels McLuhan—but makes McLuhan's Catholic-infused media analysis more secular and raw. Cronenberg was able to foretell our electronic evolution, the quasi-eucharistic way we "taste and see" the internet. The film's gore and gush might now strike us as campy, but *Videodrome* shows what happens when mind and device become one. "Death is not the end," one character says, but "the beginning of the new flesh." A curiously Catholic formulation.

Many of those influenced by McLuhan did not share his religious views; most of them weren't even aware that the media seer had deep faith. Yet McLuhan's religious sense offered structure, symbolism, and perhaps even song for his media explorations. Those persuaded by his media theories are not simultaneously persuaded by the religious vision that underpins them—yet we might consider that their attraction to a thinker so steeped in God suggests a theological osmosis of sorts. God made his way into media theory through McLuhan, whether it was recognized or not.

Rather than fading into history like many of his provocative contemporaries, McLuhan has gained traction and credibility as the years have passed. It is fascinating to realize that McLuhan only becomes *more* of a prophet the further our world turns to the digital. As Paul Levinson notes, McLuhan's metaphors were extravagant and malleable because they had to be: "In overshooting the mark, the metaphor gives the mark—and our understanding of it—room to move and grow. In contrast, definitive, fully documented descriptions of a technology, even if they are correct and thus useful in the present, may tell us little about the future."[22]

We are left to consider several questions, including, Did McLuhan have some supernatural sense? Or could his religious vision have captured some ineffable truths that both transcend the digital world and also help us comprehend it?

While McLuhan was at the end of his life, Kevin Kelly was a young photographer on freelance assignment in Jerusalem. He wandered the street at night and found himself at the Church of the Holy Sepulchre, built on the site where Jesus was crucified. Exhausted, and without a place to stay, Kelly laid down on the crucifixion spot and fell asleep. He woke when the crowd of visitors started to gather "as the sun was coming up that Easter morning, and I was staring at empty tombs."[23]

Raised Catholic, Kelly had since drifted from religious faith—until that morning. Fourteen years later, Kelly was the founding executive editor of *Wired* magazine—and Marshall McLuhan was on the masthead as the magazine's patron saint. Kelly has said that his Easter conversion resulted in, as he puts it, "a logic, comfort, leverage that I have because of that view."[24] It's a formulation that feels much like the structuring element of faith for McLuhan.

McLuhan's appearance on the masthead might be a quirk or a wink of the technology magazine's staff were it not for the faith of Kelly—and how that faith has influenced his vision of technology. Kelly has argued that "technology is actually a divine phenomenon that is a reflection of God." Technology, for Kelly, offers us another way to try to understand the impossible: at our best, we might only apprehend God as metaphor; even with all the "artificial intellects we make," we might only have "the slightest glimmer of who God is."[25]

As Katelyn Beaty described in an article for *Christianity Today*, Kelly has suggested "a technological metaphor for Jesus" based on an interaction with Jaron Lanier in 1986. The virtual reality pioneer donned goggles and gloves to enter the virtual experience, and Lanier "was completely amazed by the world he had just created." Kelly sees that moment as a "vision of the unbounded God binding himself to his creation." In an analogous way, Christ came to our world—assumed our form and failings—in order "to fix the world from the inside."[26]

Kelly had a clear supporter in the Catholic-raised Louis Rossetto, the cofounder of the magazine and the one who recruited Kelly to the editing position. Rossetto rejected the idea that *Wired* was a magazine about technology. As he wrote in a short manifesto within the first issue, the magazine "is about the most powerful people on the planet today—the Digital Generation. These are the people who not only foresaw how the merger of computers, telecommunications, and the media is transforming life at the cusp of the new millennium, they are making it happen."[27]

Wired debuted with volume 1, issue 1 in March/April 1993. On the cover, an unfocused close-up of Bruce Sterling is set against a teal background. McLuhan's name appears on the cover, advertising a conversation between Camille Paglia and Stewart Brand. On the right side of the cover, "The Medium . . ." trails off to the edge, parallel with a neon-pink tab that, if you follow the page, leads to a spread that quotes McLuhan from *The Medium Is the Massage*: "The medium, or process, of our time—electric technology—is reshaping and restructuring patterns of social interdependence and every aspect of our personal life. It is forcing us to reconsider and to re-evaluate practically every thought, every action, and every institution formerly taken for granted. Everything is changing you." The lines languidly stretch across the pages, as if McLuhan were lounging in his office sofa at the Centre for Culture and Technology.

The Brand and Paglia conversation is anchored in McLuhan's identity as a lost prophet. Paglia talks about how she was influenced by McLuhan. His books were assigned to her at Binghamton University in the mid-1960s. "What's happened to him," Paglia wonders. "Why are these people reading Lacan or Foucault who have no awareness at all of mass media? Why would anyone go on about the school of Saussure? In none of that French crap is there any reference to media. Our culture is a pop culture."[28]

Wired did its part to keep McLuhan relevant. Over the years, articles like "Honoring *Wired*'s Patron Saint," "McLuhan Lives," "Five Views of St. Marshall," and "The Wisdom of Saint Marshall, the Holy Fool" reminded readers of their guiding visionary. In one essay, contributing editor Gary Wolf concludes, "It is comforting to think McLuhan is outdated, because it alleviates our shame at not living up to his demands. His pleas for understanding and his warnings of doom are like the quaint aphoristical exhortations and eschatological prophecies of the early church."[29]

Kevin Kelly has taken McLuhan's pleas and warnings as a way to develop a "spiritual dimension to technology."[30] In Kelly's extension of McLuhan's vision, he sees the need for stewards of technology in the same way that we might see ourselves as stewards of the natural world. Kelly has argued that our nebulous, almost mystical way of talking about information sounds as if people were "talking about the Holy Spirit."[31] Technologists, Kelly observes, will place a nearly spiritual belief in information but hesitate to believe in God—more a reflection of their comfort with metaphors associated with information than any ontological truths.

Technology, Kelly believes, "can teach us about God." Technology requires attempt and failure, construction and deconstruction. "The ongoing scientific process of moving our lives away from the rule of matter and toward abstractions and intangibles can only prepare us for a better understanding of the ultimate abstraction," Kelly writes. "We tend to see God reflected in nature, but my bet is that technology is the better mirror of God."[32]

Kelly seems to describe a potential marriage of the spirit and technology that McLuhan doubted would happen but would be entirely consistent with his Christian vision. Kelly has helped McLuhan remain and evolve into our digital world. As others such as Joshua Meyrowitz have noted, "McLuhan's writing is so dense and rich that it seems to cry out for participatory exegesis and for treatment as holy text." McLuhan charged into the coming electronic world with fervor. We might consider with Meyrowitz how McLuhan's mosaics, probes, pronouncements, and even his mistakes have been "generative, rather than substantive, inspirational rather than instructional."[33] McLuhan offers us a way to reimagine the digital world through a spiritual vision of communication. The vision is not often easy, and it is not often delivered in a manner that we may like, but it is a radical and personal vision nonetheless. We would expect nothing less of a saint.

Conclusion

A Spiritual Vision for a Virtual Age

"All public Masses are hereby suspended in the Diocese of Paterson until further notice"—so went the direct and heavy message from our bishop in March 2020. "It is a moral imperative," he wrote, "for all people to do what is humanly possible to prevent the spread of the illness." No Masses. No sacrament of confirmation. No first penance, and no first Holy Communion.

Unfortunate, but unavoidable. Here in northern New Jersey, miles from an acute outbreak of Covid-19 in New York, life was put on pause. The local high school shuttered for two weeks, with students trekking to their cars while juggling overstuffed backpacks, instrument cases, and balled gym clothes. Seniors spun out of the parking lot and honked their horns, screaming as if it were the last day of school. Their metaphor became truth: it would turn out to be the last day of in-person classes for all students in the state.

A few weeks earlier, on Ash Wednesday, I had taken the train into Penn Station and then the subway into Harlem. I was lecturing on Catholic literature at Columbia University. The wind jostled the lit trees that lined the walkways on campus. The errant student and faculty member passed with smudged ashes on their forehead, a nice reminder of the day's Lenten solemnity, but I was a bit distracted by the people who wore masks. Such a sight wasn't uncommon in the city, especially on the platform waiting for a late train to arrive, but we were in the open air. It seemed like a notable start to Lent, already a funereal season.

There is a common saying at Catholic parishes: one is called to come home during Lent. It is the precipice of spring, the time of May Crowning celebrations and Easter and nostalgia. A visit with family that leads to one's first time at Mass in months, or even years, might stir some residual spirituality.

I was heartened by Romans 12:12, which the bishop shared during his message: "Rejoice in hope, endure in affliction, persevere in prayer." There's a calming rhythm to the triplicate, a stay against the growing despair. The initial response to the pandemic was slow and fractured. The most vulnerable among us were made even more so. Clearly, it would get much worse before it got better.

Soon, parishes realized that they needed to make Mass accessible to those quarantined or those nervous about traveling as cases spread across the country. Televised Mass was nothing new, but it typically meant turning to the Eternal Word Television Network (EWTN) to view Mass celebrated in the vicinity of their flagship Alabama station. Now local parishes and churches needed to decide how to approach the reality that their congregations were remote and were going to stay that way.

My family began viewing Mass streamed from the parish where my twin daughters attend Catholic school. They fashioned a prayer table full of blue, red, and wood rosaries, prayer cards dating back several decades, votive candles of Mary of Guadalupe and the sacred heart of Jesus, and a Bible. Our parish used photos of flowers and artistic renditions of Mary and Jesus as gentle transitions between the readings and homily. It was nice to see our soft-spoken priest. It felt good.

The first month or so was novel. There would be no excuses for not going to Mass. Bad weather was irrelevant. If someone in the house wasn't feeling well, they could lay down on the couch while watching. The video could be paused, rewound. The experience felt convenient—perhaps guiltily so. When the novelty wore off, when it sunk in how much we needed the environment, or perhaps the medium, of the physical church—including the ten-minute pilgrimage in the car, the air and the wind, the climbing of the steps and the opening of the door, the smells, the feel of a finger in the cool holy water, a hand curled around the end of the pew—there was an odd melancholy.

Lent's trials and Easter's epiphany can lead to a certain pensiveness during Eastertide. Christ is risen, yes, so what are we going to do about it?

It felt like a time for which Marshall McLuhan's theories and musings were made. We now had digital communion at our fingertips. So why did it feel cold to the touch?

* * *

Biblically, and liturgically, there is great spiritual value to being uncomfortable. The dissonance extends to Mass. Hardback pews? Better to help stay focused on the service than plush sofas. Kneelers that are a bit sharp on the bone? The sting might be a reminder of Christ's worn body. The priest's seemingly perpetual announcements as he holds on to the audience for another minute, and then another? A lesson in patience.

The pandemic forced many of us, like Saint Clare, to turn to screens for spiritual sustenance. Clare lived in the monastery of San Damiano for forty-two years during the early thirteenth century and was ill for more than half of that time. Sister Pacifica de Guelfuccio of Assisi, another member of Clare's monastery, testified as a witness during Clare's process of canonization that "she was so very strict in her food that the sisters marveled at how her body survived."[1] She never ate on Mondays, Wednesdays, and Fridays. On certain days, Saint Francis himself had to implore Clare to eat bread in order to retain strength. Many other witnesses affirmed the same story of her extreme abstinence. Another witness, Sister Filippa, shared the famous Christmas event of 1252, when Clare, ill and unable to attend chapel, "immediately began to hear the organ, responsories, and the entire Office of the brothers in the Church of Saint Francis, as if she were present there."[2] In the testimony of Sister Amata, she added that Clare "also saw the manger of our Lord Jesus Christ"—adding a visual component to the experience.[3]

Clare's long-term illness might cause us to wonder if she was inclined to hallucinations; when she told the sisters, "The Lord has taken good care of me because I was not able to get up from my bed," perhaps she was hearing the memory of sounds and images replayed from the past.[4] Yet the virtual experience of Clare is treated as a singular incident, a supernatural event of miraculous origin. It was not a repeated experience. When Clare was offered a virtual experience of Mass, it was a gift from God.

The metaphorical significance of the experience unfolds in *The Little Flowers of St. Francis*, written in the fourteenth century. In this telling, Christ, "willing not to leave [Clare] thus disconsolate, caused her to be miraculously carried to the church of St. Francis and to be present at the whole office of matins and of the midnight Mass, and, besides this, to receive the Holy Communion and afterward to be carried back to her bed again."[5] In this virtual communion, Clare heard and saw the Mass and ate of the Eucharist from a distance.

Although Clare was able to experience the Mass through her ears and eyes, those senses could not substitute for the sacrament. Without the Eucharist, the Mass was something akin to a pantomime or play, one that served an essential service for the bedridden Clare, but the absence was clear. As her visionary experience evolved through hagiography, the communion becomes a central element.

Early in the Covid-19 pandemic, Pope Francis suggested a spiritual communion prayer for those who were not able to partake in the Eucharist in person. Soon, the version from eighteenth-century theologian Saint Alphonsus Liguori became popular: "My Jesus, I believe that You are present in the Most Blessed Sacrament. I love You above all things, and I desire to receive You into my soul. Since I cannot now receive you sacramentally, come at least spiritually into my heart. I embrace You as if you were already there, and I unite myself wholly to You. Never permit me to be separated from You."[6] The sentiment echoes the words of Saint Teresa of Avila in *The Way of Perfection*: "When ye do not communicate, daughters, and yet hear Mass, ye may communicate spiritually, which is of very great benefit . . . for thus the love of this Lord is very much imprinted on us; for when we dispose ourselves to receive He never fails to give, after sundry ways unknown to us."[7] Perhaps digital communion could be one of these "sundry ways," an imperfect way to receive spiritual substance at a time when it was not possible to congregate together.

After some time, a curious protest began to arise in response to streamed celebrations. As one Jesuit priest from Saint Isaac Jogues Parish in Rapid City, South Dakota, noted, he "began to have misgivings" about streamed Masses when he "received a detailed set of instructions" for fitting the service "within the parameters of the broadcast." Instead of looking to "the readings or the meanings of the prayers" regarding "which eucharistic prayer to use" or "when to pause for silent reflection," such decisions were determined by the demands of the broadcast medium. The priest worried that he was being unnecessarily staid during a time that required adaptation. Yet the more he participated in these streaming Masses, he felt that such spiritual communion was "decidedly un-sacramental, even anti-sacramental." He worried that despite the good work of making Mass available to those who could not attend, it could make the parish community "dispensable."[8]

"The camera is not an inert observer," the priest argued. "It changes what we do during the liturgy, altering our perception of what Mass is." Appropriately enough, he references Marshall McLuhan in noting that the media of "bread and wine" become something else when digital: "Pictures of food and drink do not nourish. And love means remaining unsatiated with anything less than the Beloved—even when he is absent." He concluded that there "can be something salvific in that longing" for the Eucharist.[9]

It is in that space—the recognition of the paradoxical absence and presence of God in the virtual world—that we might find McLuhan's true vision.

* * *

In his fall 1971 convocation address to the University of Alberta, McLuhan observed that while "electric information has now become as indispensable to people as water to fish . . . people cannot yet accommodate to this rarefied environment." In this virtual environment, people become "discarnate data, a sort of disembodied spirit coexisting and functioning simultaneously in diverse locations, whether by telephone or by television: on the telephone, you are there, they are here." In the electronic world, we "traverse eons of human development in minutes and live in an inclusive present which assumes all pasts and futures are all one."[10]

Although McLuhan's observation was true in the age of telephone and television, it is encompassing in the virtual world. It is no longer metaphor, but matter. McLuhan's status as a prophet must come from his poetry and metaphors, from his mosaic, rather than linear, thinking. Critics of McLuhan dismiss his metaphors for their lack of materiality, and in doing so, they misunderstand McLuhan's methods. A prophet is so not because of what they get wrong but for what they get right.

In October 2016, McLuhan's own Saint Michael's College began a three-month exhibit of his work, theories, and life. The exhibit began with the unveiling of René Cera's painting *Pied Pipers All*, an interpretation of McLuhan's theories. After McLuhan's death, the mural-size painting "was sliced into three pieces and stored in a country barn" until being recovered several years later—a fitting metaphor.[11]

After the painting was unveiled, editor and critic Paul Elie gave a speech at Saint Michael's titled "The Makings of a Spirituality of Technology: Glenn Gould, Marshall McLuhan and 'Electronic Participation.'" Elie shared the notes for his speech with me, and his address sought to examine the digital space of the Catholic Church, following in the inquisitive tradition of McLuhan. Elie argues the internet is a "region" of our life—one that religious tradition helps us understand and "distinguish between literacy and immersion—to be attentive to the distinction between the way we shape it and the way it shapes us."[12] Religious tradition can help us discern between those digital experiences that are helpful and harmful.

Antonio Spadaro, SJ, the Italian theologian and Jesuit priest who Elie ponders in his speech, offers some instruction on the former option—how a cybertheology might

be useful. Spadaro views the internet to be "an anthropo-
logical space that is deeply intertwined with our everyday
lives. Instead of making us leave our world to delve into the
virtual world, technology has made the digital world penetrate our ordinary world."[13] Our human "contacts" online
should be "harmonized and integrated into a life of full,
sincere relationships."[14]

The synthesis of the real and the virtual causes us to
reconsider the Christian vision of liturgy and sacrament.
Spadaro reminds us that at its core, "Christianity is a com-
municative event." He draws a contrast between Mark
16:15, when Christ tells us to "go into the whole world and
proclaim the gospel to every creature," and Exodus 20:4,
which "put us on our guard against making images, from a
technology that substantially exposes idolatry."[15]

This presents a problem. Spadaro recognizes that in the
virtual world, "the Church finds itself being stressed by a
logic of connections that, ultimately, will help her to understand more profoundly her nature as a universal instrument of reconciliation and communion."[16] In the same way
that Christian theology and faith practice had to reckon
with the shift from oral to print culture, and from manual
copying to mechanical reproduction, the Church and its
believers must engage with the evolution of our mediums
of communication and their resulting environments.

Yet at the same time, echoing McLuhan's most acute
moments of societal skepticism, Spadaro warns, "The
Church cannot embrace a logic that, ultimately, is exposed
to the domain that knows how to manipulate public opinion."[17] In 2002, the Pontifical Council for Social Communications took a certain stance on these concerns in

"The Church and the Internet." The council affirms Pope Paul VI's worry that the Church "would feel guilty before the Lord" if it did not embrace the evangelizing possibilities of media.[18] The internet offers "direct and immediate access to important religious and spiritual resources" and has "a remarkable capacity to overcome distance and isolation, bringing people into contact with like-minded persons of good will who join in virtual communities of faith to encourage and support one another."[19]

Despite the internet's potential for uniting the isolated and disparate, the council concludes that virtual communion is unable to capture "the incarnational reality of the sacraments and the liturgy." Ultimately, "there are no sacraments on the Internet; and even the religious experiences possible there by the grace of God are insufficient apart from real-world interaction with other persons of faith." At its best, the council argues, the virtual world should be seen as a way to extend the liturgy to those who are unable to experience it in person and to bring others into the "true community" of in-person celebration. Justice and temperance are essential to ensuring that the virtual world is a place of goodwill; for the Church, merely "hanging back timidly from fear of technology or some other reason is not acceptable."[20]

Spadaro offers some useful ways to engage the internet as an environment. The virtual rather than real existence of the internet makes it a constantly evolving, potentially subversive medium. We might begin by remembering that the screen, the way that we encounter this virtual world, is not the originator of the information continued therein but its temporary medium: "Whoever looks at the screen does not look through it but into it, and so what he sees is always an apparition and not a view or a vision. . . . We do not see things but realities that appear at a determined moment, and whose visibility is neither stable nor guaranteed."[21]

Virtual events, whether personal or public, are "a spectacle of sorts." Even more confounding are events—whether they are broadcasts, posts, tweets, or even texts—that originate and unfold fully virtually. For such experiences, the "landscape—that is, the panorama that is beyond perception and contemplating in which we recognize the landscape—becomes a *simulacra*, that is, an image that has no corresponding reality, of an environment or its own true inscape, namely an interiorized panorama inside of which the mystery is brought back."[22] A fully virtual sacrament, then, becomes problematic.

Spadaro's own argument builds toward a thesis that centers the theories of Teilhard de Chardin as a more sacramental counter to the intriguing secular arguments of Pierre Lévy, the French philosopher and media theorist. Spadaro hesitates to follow Lévy's vision, since for the theorist, "God is transmuted into an open possibility for human development; the angelic or celestial world becomes the region of the virtual worlds, through which human beings are in *intellectual collectivity*; the intellect becomes the space for the communication and navigation of individual members of the collective intelligence." Echoing the earlier recommendations of the Vatican council, Spadaro worries that an unregulated virtual space can mean a well-intentioned "communal intelligence" that can become "a collectivist and depersonalized utopia," where God molds to the whims of the beholder.[23]

While he acknowledges that Teilhard "did not resolve some of the shadows and ambiguities" of the impending Omega Point of collective, virtual experience, he thinks the Jesuit paleontologist was not merely prescient but prophetic. As previously noted in this book, McLuhan was certainly influenced by Teilhard—even if he hesitated to fully acknowledge so in his speeches and writings—but Teilhard's theories were developed in a world on the precipice of electronic formulation rather than digital transcendence. When Teilhard died in 1955, McLuhan was just beginning to shift his thinking from print to television.

Although Teilhard is essential to this conversation, McLuhan is the more apt model for understanding contemporary communication. It is precisely because McLuhan's theories were so centrally Catholic and yet doctrinally undetectable to many that he is the perfect model for a spiritual understanding of the virtual world. While more cynical critics might think McLuhan's method was a form of obfuscation, it is better to consider that McLuhan's Christian vision so fully formed his worldview that there was no need to outline the foundational theologies or doctrines that structured his assumptions. McLuhan's role was not to be an evangelist; it was to describe the changing world that he occupied and to inevitably do so as a Christian. In a secular world, that itself is significant.

* * *

I am the youngest child in my family. One recurring experience from my childhood went like this: I am rummaging through boxes and bins stored in the basement (and if I am feeling especially adventurous, the attic) and discover stacks of photographs of my older siblings from the 1970s. Trips to the zoo, amusement parks, and lakes were arranged among shots from football, basketball, and softball games. I would sit in the near dark and shift through the collections that depicted a world before my life—a phantom childhood, in a way.

What is the reason for taking a photograph? It is the type of question that McLuhan would ask, an ostensibly simple question that forces us to uncover assumptions and places us within a broader system. I know the purpose of many photographs now, in a virtual world: it is often to share, and possibly promote, a version of ourselves. It is not an entirely inaccurate version, but it is a snippet or segment of that fuller version.

More specifically, what was the purpose of taking a photograph in 1973? It was to capture a moment, of course—in recognition that moments are fleeting and that memory is imperfect. We fear that our life will pass by and vanish, that we will vanish along with it. A photograph taken in 1973 might have been shared with someone else: perhaps my mom shared a photo of my sister standing in front of a giraffe with my aunt living in Virginia, or it might have remained in our own house, only to be unearthed as part of a swell of nostalgia.

Yet other than a Polaroid photograph—which, in some ways, distorted an image through color and focus, even if it offered us that image immediately—we had to wait for photographs to be developed. Our real time continued without the loop of sharing, reaction, and response. In the same way that it is difficult to explain social media to someone who rarely uses the internet, we also might wonder how to explain and capture this feeling of revisiting life on our walk back from a photo store counter. The opening of the envelope flap, the shuffling through photos to see if they are focused or grainy. The worry that a bad shot would mean a moment missed forever.

What if the reason for a photograph was to extend our life? To offer another medium to our existence, a simultaneous copy or continuation? "The present and the future now coexist at the same time," Douglas Coupland said in 2016, well into the virtual age. "It's why time doesn't feel like time any more. We're inside the future."[24] Those photographs that I found in the basement were a distinct moment in the lives of my siblings, who were and are still alive—so that the photograph is both them and not, a representation and a distortion.

McLuhan knew that the virtual age would mean an extreme present, a disruption of time that is antithetical to a print world, where pagination and narrative create a sense of profluence. The present and the past are now simultaneous because they can both be streamed simultaneously.

What does this matter for the world of the spirit? Does it matter? What is the purpose of a spiritual vision for the internet? Spadaro is correct that the virtual world will continue with or without our concern for its spirit, and to ignore that region, as Elie says, is to allow it to descend into frightful places. Marshall McLuhan is not here to help us, but all lives are eternal in the virtual world. In the spirit of Father John Culkin's distillation of McLuhan's theories into a "barbarously brief form," here are five postulates of a spiritual vision for the internet.

1. In the Virtual World, There Is Only the Present

Traditional storytelling assumes a structure of profluence—not merely the existence of a beginning, middle, and end but an inherent energy to a story that flows like a river's current toward a location in the distance. Even experimental storytelling that subverts this structure, such as Eugène Ionesco's Theater of the Absurd, does so with an assumption of tradition as the parodic origin. The only traditional senses of storytelling—and therefore time—in the virtual world are the ones that we bring to the experience, not inherent from the virtual world itself. Coupland, following McLuhan, recognizes that the global village is both an experiential and temporal phenomenon. The internal energy of the virtual world arises from the fact that all experiences are present in that their temporality is defined by the parameters of our experience. Online, there is no morning, afternoon, or evening. Yet this runs counter to the world in which our physical bodies inhabit. Biologically and socially, we know there is a sunrise and sunset. We know that we have been born and that we will die. This tension can stretch us apart; we must never fully operate on virtual time, as it can be disastrous to our spirit and mind.

2. To Be on the Internet Is Not to Be of the Internet

Once again, it helps if we remember how Marshall McLuhan clarified his most famous dictum, "the medium is the message": "It really means a hidden environment of services created by an innovation, and the hidden environment of services is the thing that changes people. It is the environment that changes people, not the technology."[25] Twitter does not change us, but it is the environment created by the technology of Twitter that distorts us, for even in performing for that world, we are straying from our instincts. Social media rewards provocation and personae—the exaggeration of self. The more time one spends saturated within such an environment, the more that those modes of being appear natural, or at least can become rationalized. It has become a joke to mock those who announce their pending hibernations from social media only to send a smattering of posts hours later, but their intentions show the unrest of being on the internet. Our metaphors often reveal our unconscious truths, and the connotation of *maintaining* an online presence demonstrates the technical attention necessary to this calibration. Even casual or ironic participation in conspiratorial thinking online—where one is rewarded for tribalism, partisanship, and indulging in caricature—opens the door to earnest acceptance of those actions. Writers and artists, those who tell the stories of our culture, must be especially wary of how the performance of being online neuters creation. This performance can disrupt provocative and experimental creation—exactly the type of work that complicates assumptions and reveals hidden truths. The promotion and presence of being online infect the mental space of creation, which requires contemplation and authenticity. It can be nothing short of a spiritual scandal.

3. Virtual Communion Can Lessen Isolation

Following the bedridden experiences of Saint Clare, and considering the incredible accessibility needed during the

Covid-19 pandemic, we should acknowledge that communing virtually can do wonders to lessen the mental, social, and spiritual effects of isolation. The pandemic laid bare issues that many have been struggling with for their entire lives: the feeling that they are disparate from the world and are unable to participate in the union of believers. In many instances, faith communities needed to create these virtual spaces in the rush of the early months of 2020, when the mysterious disease was spreading across the world. In the time since, many have refined their delivery and approach and should be commended for bringing the electronic and digital Word to their congregations. Now we need to delve deeper—theologically and personally—into how a sense of virtual communion could unearth the best parts of McLuhan's "global village" and how we might temper those moments when to be online often means to be our worst selves. Nearly a hundred years ago, when Vatican Radio was established following the signing of the Lateran Pacts in February 1929, Pope Pius XI offered his blessing for the new medium: "Bless this series of machines that serve to transmit into the waves of the ether so that, communicating the apostolic word even to peoples far away, we will be united with you in one family."[26] We should embrace this blessing as a call to action.

4. We Must Reimagine the Sacraments in a Virtual World

In *Christus Vivit*, his exhortation to young Catholics, Pope Francis wrote of Carlo Acutis, an Italian boy who died of leukemia at fifteen in 2006. "Carlo was well aware that the whole apparatus of communications, advertising and social networking can be used to lull us, to make us addicted to consumerism and buying the latest thing on the market, obsessed with our free time, caught up in negativity," Francis wrote. "Yet he knew how to use the new communications technology to transmit the Gospel, to communicate values and beauty."[27] During his young life, the programming-adept Acutis cataloged miracles, grounded by his own eucharistic devotion. He was beatified in 2020, paving the way for the "first millennial saint." We might uphold the life and inspiration of this likely saint against the reasonable concerns of theologians like Spadaro. "The fundamental risk that seems joined to the experience of the liturgy on the Web is that of a flow of 'magic' that is able to fade away," he worries, "until the sense of community and ecclesial mediation that is incarnated is canceled, so as to exalt instead the role of the technology that makes the event possible."[28] These are important concerns. Yet in times both extraordinary and ordinary, we must reimagine the presence of Christ in a virtual world. If we accept that the virtual world is a base place where sacredness could never exist, then that grace will never be so. When McLuhan warned Jacques Maritain that "the Prince of this World is a very great electric engineer," his context was the concern that electronic *connection* would replace electronic *communion*. McLuhan, much like Spadaro, worried about the "illusion of the world as spiritual substance."[29] Any extension of the sacramental experience must be aware of these possibilities—but to not consider a new imagination of communion might be forfeiting souls to the same Prince of the World whom McLuhan feared. The project will be challenging and constant, but if we value the sacraments, then it is an absolutely necessary one.

5. We Must Transcend the Obsolescence

Our time in this world is temporary. In the spirit of McLuhan's training and foundation as a scholar of literature, we might end with how that medium can help us transcend our inevitable obsolescence. In Wallace Stevens's poem "Of Modern Poetry," he notes that "the theatre" of poetry, art, and experience "was changed / To something else."[30] The past and tradition had become a "souvenir." Now we must "learn the speech of the place" and "construct a new stage." Our communication must reach the "delicatest ear of the mind" of our "invisible audience"— which is not listening to the "play" that we perform, "but to itself." In the virtual world, we are a "metaphysician in the dark." We might even be sacramental, as we are "twanging a wiry string that gives / Sounds passing through sudden rightnesses." Stevens recognizes that the modern poem is a "poem of the act of the mind," and yet he affirmed elsewhere that "God and the imagination are one."[31] In order to transcend the inevitable obsolescence of our mediums, and ourselves, we must find the eternal, nourish it, and share that sustenance. Only then might our extreme virtual present become something real, and something wonderful.

With a sense of humor that McLuhan himself would appreciate, Douglas Coupland notes that McLuhan "was, truth be told, an illogical and fusty old vehicle for new ideas, and some people couldn't (and still can't) reconcile Marshall's appearance with what came out of his mouth."[32]

And yet Coupland's admiration for McLuhan is recognition that we don't get to choose our prophets—and that the people who have a gift for perception are not always the ones who are the most convenient to our ideologies. The Catholic underpinnings of McLuhan's perception, as well as his hope that a sense of virtual communion could overtake the negative elements of the global village, make him an especially apt prophet in an anatheist world—a place where many seek God after God.

The electronic world—and even more so, the virtual world—makes us all disembodied and discarnate. In a way, we become angels, as McLuhan thought. We are more than our bodies. Online, we are all soul. Imagine what might happen if we acted commensurate with that spirit. McLuhan's theories offer us a guide. His theories arrived, and remain, as poetic mosaics, ponderings, and paradoxes. Structurally, they are challenging; intellectually, they are revelatory. The route we must take to achieve digital communion is not easy nor direct, but faith never is—and the result might feel like grace.

Acknowledgments

Sections of this book previously appeared in different forms in *America* and *The Millions*. I appreciate the support of those editors.

Gratitude to my parents and family. Many thanks to my editor, Emily King, and the entire team at Fortress Press.

Olivia, Amelia, and Jennifer: I love you. Everything that I write is for each of you.

Notes

Preface

1 "Pope's Mass Ticket Calls Swamp Yanks," *Los Angeles Times*, September 29, 1965, B5.

2 "Pope's N.Y. Trip Held 'a Risk Worth Taking,'" *Los Angeles Times*, September 24, 1965, 12.

3 "An Apostle on the Move Arrives," *Los Angeles Times*, October 4, 1965, A4.

4 "N.Y. Is Told to See Pope on T.V.," *New York Times*, September 29, 1965, 1.

5 Martin Arnold, "It's Almost as If They Were All in Church," *New York Times*, October 5, 1965, SU4_4.

6 Robert J. Donovan, "New York Bustles with Preparations for Pope," *Los Angeles Times*, October 3, 1965, E1.

7 Arthur Gelb, *City Room* (New York: Berkeley Books, 2003), 415.

8 David W. Dunlap, "Here's the Pope. Where's the Paper?," *New York Times*,

July 10, 2015, https://www.nytimes.com/times-insider/2015/07/10/1965-heres-the-pope-wheres-the-paper/.

9 Dunlap.

10 Gelb, *City Room*, 418.

11 "A Day in Pope's Visit," *Broadcasting*, October 4, 1965, 75.

12 Jack Gould, "TV: Coverage of Pope Paul VI Visit Readied," *New York Times*, October 1, 1965, SU3_1.

13 "Millions See Pope's Visit as Presented Live by TV," *New York Times*, October 5, 1965, 2.

14 Quoted in *Catholic Standard and Times*, October 8, 1965, 6.

15 "Pope Will Say Mass in Latin at Yankee Stadium," *New York Times*, October 2, 1965, SUA2_3.

16 Murray Kempton, "The Pope among Us," *New Republic*, September 21, 1965.

17 William E. Farrell, "Ninety Thousand Amens," *New York Times*, October 5, 1965, SU2_1.

18 Marshall McLuhan, *The Medium and the Light: Reflections on Religion*, ed. Eric McLuhan and Jacek Szklarek (Eugene, OR: Wipf & Stock, 2010), xxv.

19 Gerald Emanuel Stearn, ed., *McLuhan: Hot and Cool* (New York: Signet Books, 1969), 31.

20 Stearn, 32.

21 *Take 30*, CBC, April 1, 1965, with hosts George Garlock and Paul Soles.

22 Marshall McLuhan, *Letters of Marshall McLuhan*, ed. Matie Molinaro, Corinne McLuhan, and William Toye

23 Alexander Ross, "The High Priest of Pop Culture," *Maclean's*, July 3, 1965, 13.

24 Ross, 13.

25 Friden advertisement, *Time*, April 8, 1966, 87.

26 Marshall McLuhan and Quentin Fiore, *The Medium Is the Massage* (Corte Madera, CA: Gingko Press, 2001), 146.

27 "Color TV Commercials to Promote Religion," *New York Times*, January 23, 1966, 69.

28 McLuhan, *Medium and Light*, xxvi.

Introduction

1 McLuhan, *Medium and Light*, 59.

2 McLuhan, 60.

3 John M. Culkin, SJ, "A Schoolman's Guide to Marshall McLuhan," *Saturday Review*, March 18, 1967, 53.

4 Culkin, 72.

5 McLuhan, *Letters*, 1.

6 McLuhan, *Medium and Light*, ix.

7 Janine Marchessault, *Marshall McLuhan: Cosmic Media* (London: Sage, 2005), 6.

8 W. Terrence Gordon, *Marshall McLuhan: Escape into Understanding* (New York: Basic Books, 1997), 54.

9 McLuhan, *Letters*, 4.

10 Marchessault, *Marshall*, 4.

11 McLuhan, *Letters*, 6.

12 McLuhan, 29.

13 McLuhan, 41.

14 McLuhan, 72.

15 McLuhan, 73.

16 McLuhan, 73.

17 McLuhan, 74.

18 McLuhan, 75.

19 Gordon, *McLuhan*, 47.

20 Gordon, 54.

21 Stearn, *McLuhan*, xiv.

22 McLuhan, *Letters*, 10.

23 Marshall McLuhan, "G. K. Chesterton: A Practical Mystic," *Dalhousie Review* 15 (1936): 462.

24 McLuhan, 455.

25 McLuhan, 458.

26 McLuhan, *Letters*, 74.

27 McLuhan, 42.

28 Marshall McLuhan, *The Interior Landscape: The Literary Criticism of Marshall McLuhan*, ed. Eugene McNamara (Toronto: McGraw-Hill, 1969), xiii.

29 McLuhan, xiv.

30 McLuhan, *Letters*, 108.

31 Marshall McLuhan, "The Analogical Mirrors," *Kenyon Review*, Summer 1944, 322.

32 McLuhan, 325.

33 McLuhan, 331.

34 Marshall McLuhan, *Culture Is Our Business* (New York: Ballantine Books, 1970), 270.

35 McLuhan, *Medium and Light*, 35.

36 Marshall McLuhan and Harley Parker, *Through the Vanishing Point: Space in Poetry and Painting* (New York: Harper & Row, 1968), 210.

37 McLuhan and Parker, 179.

38 Marshall McLuhan, "Gerard Hopkins and His World," *New York Times*, September 3, 1944, BR7.

39 McLuhan, *Letters*, 82.

40 McLuhan, 83.

41 John Whitney Evans, "Making the Best of a Bad Job? Newman Chaplains between the Code and the Council," *U.S. Catholic Historian* 11, no. 1 (Winter 1993): 41.

42 McLuhan, *Letters*, 99.

43 McLuhan, 100.

44 McLuhan, 102.

45 McLuhan, 180.
46 McLuhan, 180.
47 McLuhan, 384.
48 McLuhan, 369.
49 McLuhan, 362.
50 McLuhan, *Medium and Light*, xvii.
51 McLuhan, 103.
52 McLuhan, *Letters*, 394.
53 McLuhan, *Medium and Light*, 82.
54 McLuhan, 45.
55 McLuhan, 50.
56 McLuhan, 144.
57 McLuhan, 142.
58 McLuhan, 145.
59 McLuhan, 143.
60 McLuhan, 110.
61 McLuhan, *Medium and Light*, 145.
62 McLuhan, *Letters*, 480.
63 McLuhan, *Medium and Light*, 148.
64 McLuhan, *Letters*, 480.

65 McLuhan, 480.
66 McLuhan, *Medium and Light*, 114.
67 McLuhan, 86.
68 McLuhan, *Letters*, 370.
69 McLuhan, 387.
70 McLuhan, *Medium and Light*, 209.
71 McLuhan, 146.
72 McLuhan, *Letters*, 368.
73 McLuhan, 399.
74 McLuhan, 479.
75 McLuhan, *Medium and Light*, 147.
76 McLuhan, xvii.
77 McLuhan, 64.
78 McLuhan, xxiv.
79 McLuhan, xxvii.
80 McLuhan, 104.
81 McLuhan, 55.
82 McLuhan, 64–65.
83 McLuhan, 86.
84 McLuhan, 174.

Chapter 1

1 Edmund Carpenter and Marshall McLuhan, eds., *Explorations in Communication* (Boston: Beacon Press, 1960), 208.
2 Marshall McLuhan, *The Gutenberg Galaxy* (Toronto: University of Toronto Press, 1962), 1.
3 McLuhan, n.p.
4 S. H. Steinberg, *Five Hundred Years of Printing* (London: British Library, 1996), 5.
5 John Man, *Gutenberg: How One Man Remade the World* (New York: John Wiley & Sons, 2002), 89.
6 Man, 89.
7 Man, 89.
8 Man, 91.
9 Man, 115.
10 Man, 160.
11 Leonard Dudley, *Information Revolutions in the History of the West* (Cheltenham, UK: Edward Elgar, 2008), 77.
12 David E. Wellbery and Judith Ryan, eds., *A New History of German Literature* (Cambridge, MA: Harvard University Press, 2004), 1457.
13 Steinberg, *Five Hundred Years*, 1.
14 Steinberg, 63.
15 Elizabeth L. Eisenstein, *The Printing Press as an Agent of Change* (Cambridge:

Cambridge University Press, 1979), 80.
16 John 21:25.
17 David Lyle Jeffrey, ed., *A Dictionary of Biblical Tradition in English Literature* (Grand Rapids: Eerdmans, 1992), 102.
18 Raymond J. Nogar, OP, *The Lord of the Absurd* (New York: Herder & Herder, 1966), 24.
19 Ps 139:16.
20 Isa 29:11.
21 Ezek 2:7.
22 Ezek 2:9–10.
23 Quoted in Jeffrey, *Dictionary*, 100–101.
24 Simon Eliot and Jonathan Rose, eds., *A Companion to the History of the Book* (Oxford: Blackwell, 2007), 195.
25 Carpenter and McLuhan, *Explorations*, 129.
26 Marshall McLuhan, interview by Eric Norden, *Playboy*, March 1969, 72, available at https://nextnature.net/2009/12/the-playboy-interview-marshall-mcluhan.
27 McLuhan, *Galaxy*, 47.
28 McLuhan, 104.
29 McLuhan, 126.
30 McLuhan, 141.

31 McLuhan, 144.
32 McLuhan, 157.
33 McLuhan, 3.
34 McLuhan, 72.
35 McLuhan, 5.
36 Marshall McLuhan, *Understanding Media* (Cambridge, MA: MIT Press, 1994), 3–4.
37 McLuhan, 45.
38 McLuhan, 5.
39 McLuhan, 47.
40 McLuhan, 57.
41 McLuhan, 61.
42 McLuhan, 80.
43 Pierre Teilhard de Chardin, *The Making of a Mind*, trans. René Hague (New York: Harper & Row, 1965), 281.
44 Pierre Teilhard de Chardin, *The Phenomenon of Man* (New York: Harper & Row, 1965), 240.
45 McLuhan, *Galaxy*, 32.
46 Nogar, *Lord of the Absurd*, 119.
47 Nogar, 121.
48 Nogar, 124.
49 Nogar, 125–26.
50 Nogar, 140.
51 McLuhan, *Galaxy*, 46.
52 McLuhan, 135.
53 McLuhan, *Understanding Media*, 248.
54 Jennifer Cobb Kreisberg, "A Globe, Clothing Itself with a Brain," *Wired*, June 1995, https://www.wired.com/1995/06/teilhard/.
55 McLuhan, *Medium and Light*, 47.
56 McLuhan, *Galaxy*, 276.

Chapter 2

1 McLuhan, *Letters*, 18.
2 McLuhan, 37.
3 McLuhan, 78.
4 McLuhan and Parker, *Vanishing*, 245.
5 McLuhan, *Galaxy*, 334.
6 McLuhan, 334.
7 McLuhan, *Interior*, 33.
8 McLuhan, *Galaxy*, 217.
9 McLuhan, 201.
10 Quotations throughout come from the version of the dissertation that was eventually published, Marshall McLuhan, *The Place of Thomas Nashe in the Learning of His Time*, ed. W. Terrence Gordon (Corte Madera, CA: Gingko Press, 2006), 16.
11 McLuhan, 7.
12 McLuhan, 50.
13 Quoted by the volume editor in McLuhan, 57.
14 McLuhan, 201.
15 McLuhan, 209.
16 McLuhan, 241.
17 Phoebe Sheavyn, *The Literary Profession in the Elizabethan Age* (Manchester: Manchester University Press, 1967), 105.
18 McLuhan, *Nashe*, 253.
19 Alan Jacobs, "Why Bother with Marshall McLuhan?," *New Atlantis*, no. 31 (Spring 2011): 125.
20 McLuhan, *Understanding Media*, 54.
21 Lawrence Laurent, "Canadian Scholar Stir Controversy," *Washington Post*, April 5, 1966, B4.
22 McLuhan, *Medium and Light*, 170.
23 McLuhan, *Letters*, 183.
24 McLuhan, 189.
25 Keith B. Williams, "Time and Motion Studies: Joycean Cinematicity in *A Portrait of the Artist as a Young Man*," in *Cinematicity in Media History*, ed. Jeffrey Geiger and Karin Littau (Edinburgh: Edinburgh University Press, 2013), 88–106.
26 McLuhan, *Interior*, xiv.
27 McLuhan, *Mechanical*, 3.
28 McLuhan, 4.
29 McLuhan, 59.
30 McLuhan, *Interior*, 23.
31 McLuhan, *Galaxy*, 267.
32 McLuhan, 74.
33 Kevin Rockett, Luke Gibbons, and John Hill, *Cinema and Ireland* (London: Routledge, 1987), 4.
34 Williams, "Time and Motion Studies," 88.
35 Williams, 90.
36 Williams, 94.
37 James Joyce, *Ulysses* (New York: Vintage Books, 1986), 31.
38 Joyce, 38.

39 McLuhan, *Galaxy*, 83.

40 Donald F. Theall, *James Joyce's Techno-Poetics* (Toronto: University of Toronto Press, 1997), 15.

41 Theall, 15.

42 Theall, 105.

43 Theall, 109.

44 Donald Theall, "Beyond the Orality/Literacy Principle: James Joyce and the Pre-history of Cyberspace," *Postmodern Culture* 2, no. 3 (May 1992): 5, http://pmc.iath.virginia.edu/text-only/issue.592/theall.592.

45 McLuhan, *Letters*, 298.

46 McLuhan, *Mechanical*, 101.

47 McLuhan, *Galaxy*, 269.

48 McLuhan, *Interior*, 24.

49 McLuhan, 25.

50 Quoted in Richard Ellman, *James Joyce* (Oxford: Oxford University Press, 1965), 27.

51 McLuhan, *Interior*, 34.

52 McLuhan, 37–38.

53 McLuhan, 46.

54 William Carlos Williams, "A Note on the Recent Work of James Joyce," *Transition*, no. 8 (November 1927): 153.

55 Timothy Leary, "The Laughing Religion," *East Village Other*, August 19–September 1, 1967, 10.

56 Lance Strate, "Drugs: The Intensions of Humanity," in *Drugs & Media: New Perspectives on Communication, Consumption, and Consciousness*, ed. Robert C. MacDougall (New York: Continuum, 2012), 19.

57 Roger Barton, *Media in Advertising* (New York: McGraw-Hill, 1964), 227.

58 *Computerworld*, June 21, 1967, 1.

Chapter 3

1 "Far-off Speakers Seen as Well as Heard Here in a Test of Television," *New York Times*, April 8, 1927, 1.

2 "Far-off," 20.

3 "Far-off," 1.

4 "Far-off," 1.

5 *Bell Laboratories Record* 4, no. 3 (May 1927): 301.

6 John Dennis Anderson, "The Medium Is the Mother: Elsie McLuhan, Elocution, and Her Son Marshall," *Text and Performance Quarterly* 37, no. 2 (September 2017): 112.

7 Douglas Coupland, *Marshall McLuhan: You Know Nothing of My Work!* (New York: Atlas, 2011), 27.

8 Stearn, *McLuhan*, xii.

9 Marshall McLuhan, *The Mechanical Bride: Folklore of Industrial Man* (London: Duckworth Overlook, 2011), 101.

10 McLuhan and Fiore, *Massage*, 63.

11 "Television," *New York Times*, April 8, 1927, 22.

12 W. B. Yeats, *Ideas of Good and Evil* (New York: Macmillan, 1903), 243.

13 Yeats, 245.

14 Yeats, 247.

15 Yeats, 247.

16 Yeats, 248.

17 Yeats, 249.

18 Marshall McLuhan, "The Southern Quality," *Sewanee Review* 55, no. 3 (July–September 1947): 362.

19 McLuhan, 363.

20 Marshall McLuhan, *From Cliché to Archetype* (New York: Pocket Books, 1971), 20.

21 McLuhan, 64.

22 McLuhan, 118.

23 McLuhan, 140.

24 McLuhan, 150.

25 W. B. Yeats, *The Collected Works of W. B. Yeats*, vol. 10, *Later Articles and Reviews*, ed. Colton Johnson (New York: Scribner, 2000), 224.

26 McLuhan, *Cliché*, 149.

27 McLuhan, *Mechanical*, v.

28 McLuhan, v.

29 Coupland, *McLuhan*, 58.

30 Coupland, 58.

31 Coupland, 112.

32 McLuhan, *Mechanical*, 75.

33 McLuhan, 50.

34 McLuhan, 80.

35 McLuhan, 81.

36 McLuhan, 156.
37 Marshall McLuhan, "Myth and Mass Media," *Daedalus* 88, no. 2 (Spring 1959): 346.
38 McLuhan, 344.
39 McLuhan, 345.
40 Pope Pius XII, *Miranda Prorsus*, September 1, 1957, http://www.vatican.va/content/pius-xii/en/encyclicals/documents/hf_p-xii_enc_08091957_miranda-prorsus.html.
41 Pius.
42 Pope Pius XII, *Lettre Apostolique Proclamant Ste. Claire Patronne Céleste de la Télévision*, February 14, 1957, available at https://www.vatican.va/content/pius-xii/fr/apost_letters/documents/hf_p-xii_apl_21081958_st-claire.html.
43 McLuhan, *Letters*, 227.
44 McLuhan, 227.
45 McLuhan, 251.
46 "People Are Talking About . . . ," *Vogue*, July 1, 1966, 60.
47 Marshall McLuhan, "Great Change-Overs for You," *Vogue*, July 1, 1966, 62.
48 McLuhan, 62.

49 Aleene MacMinn, "McLuhan in California," *Los Angeles Times*, April 16, 1967, C1.
50 MacMinn, 12.
51 Philip Marchand, *Marshall McLuhan: The Medium and the Messenger* (New York: Ticknor & Fields, 1989), 182.
52 Eileen Lottman, "Under Covers," *Village Voice*, December 6, 1973, 30.
53 Adam Michaels and Jeffrey T. Schnapp, *The Electric Information Age Book* (New York: Princeton Architectural Press, 2012), 49.
54 Michaels and Schnapp, 39.
55 Michaels and Schnapp, 49.
56 Michaels and Schnapp, 55.
57 Michaels and Schnapp, 70.
58 Michaels and Schnapp, 72.
59 Marvin Kitman, "Get the Message?," *New York Times*, March 26, 1967, 268.
60 Michaels and Schnapp, *Electric*, 87.
61 McLuhan and Fiore, *Massage*, 125.
62 McLuhan, interview by Norden.
63 McLuhan.
64 McLuhan.

Chapter 4

1 Frank Quigley, "McLuhan at Fordham despite Legal Problems," *Fordham Ram*, September 19, 1967, 1.
2 Marshall McLuhan, Harley Parker, and Ted Carpenter, "The Technological Unconscious (Inauguration/Opening Lecture)," introd. John Culkin, September 18, 1967, Fordham University, Bronx, New York, YouTube video, 42:02, https://www.youtube.com/watch?v=WfnHB5f6FZM.
3 Wallace Turner, "Understanding M'Luhan, by Him," *New York Times*, November 22, 1966, 43.
4 "Controversial Professor Gives First Fordham Talk," *Times Record*, September 19, 1967, 1.
5 Frank Quigley, "$100,000 Chair Going to Toronto Professor," *Fordham Ram*, January 6, 1967, 1.
6 Edward Cowan, "McLuhan Calls Work on Media Lonely," *New York Times*, October 5, 1970, 10.

7 McLuhan, Parker, and Carpenter, "Technological Unconscious."
8 Marshall McLuhan, "Roles, Masks, and Performances," *New Literary History* 2, no. 3 (Spring 1971): 528.
9 McLuhan, *Galaxy*, 31.
10 McLuhan, *Letters*, 245.
11 McLuhan, 253.
12 McLuhan, 261.
13 McLuhan, 278.
14 McLuhan, 332.
15 Harry J. Skornia, "Understanding Media Application (Draft)," January 1959, 1, found in the collected correspondence between the National Association of Educational Broadcasters and Marshall McLuhan, July to December 1959, https://archive.org/details/naeb-b066-f10 (hereafter, NAEB and McLuhan correspondence).
16 Marshall McLuhan, letter to Harry J. Skornia, December 16, 1958, 2, NAEB and McLuhan correspondence.

17 McLuhan, 2.
18 Marshall McLuhan, "Project in Understanding New Media (Overview)," NAEB and McLuhan correspondence.
19 Marshall McLuhan, *Report on Project in Understanding New Media*, 1960, 3–4, NAEB and McLuhan correspondence.
20 McLuhan, 3.
21 Marshall McLuhan, "The Electric Culture," *Renascence* 13, no. 4 (Summer 1961): 220.
22 McLuhan, *Galaxy*, 5.
23 McLuhan, 30.
24 Walter J. Ong, SJ, *The Presence of the Word: Some Prolegomena for Cultural and Religious History* (New Haven, CT: Yale University Press, 1967), 7.
25 Marshall McLuhan, "The Agenbite of Outwit," 1963, available at http://projects.chass.utoronto.ca/mcluhan-studies/v1_iss2/1_2art6.htm.
26 McLuhan.
27 McLuhan, *Understanding Media*, 4–5.
28 McLuhan, 57.
29 McLuhan, 61.
30 McLuhan, 80.
31 Marshall McLuhan, "The Future of Man in the Electric Age," BBC, 1965, available at http://www.marshallmcluhanspeaks.com/interview/1965-the-future-of-man-in-the-electric-age/index.html.
32 McLuhan, "Great Change-Overs," 62–63.
33 McLuhan, 115.
34 Stearn, *McLuhan*, 272.
35 Stearn, 287.
36 McLuhan, interview by Norden.
37 John M. Culkin, SJ, "A Churchman's Guide to Marshall McLuhan," *Religious Education* 63, no. 6 (November–December 1968): 461.
38 *The Mike McManus Show*, TV Ontario, 1977, available at https://www.marshallmcluhanspeaks.com/interview/1977-violence-as-a-quest-for-identity/index.html.
39 Thomas Pynchon, *The Crying of Lot 49* (New York: Harper Perennial, 1999), 14.

40 Pynchon, 14.
41 Culkin, "Churchman's," 457.
42 Culkin, 461.
43 Culkin, 461.
44 Culkin, 462.
45 Austin Flannery, OP, ed., *Vatican II: The Conciliar and Post Conciliar Documents* (Northport, NY: Costello, 1975), 291.
46 Quoted in Flannery, 296.
47 Flannery, 297.
48 Flannery, 340.
49 Flannery, 341.
50 McLuhan, *Understanding Media*, 20.
51 Ronald A. Sarno, *Using Media in Religious Education* (Birmingham, AL: Religious Education Press, 1987), 107.
52 Derrick de Kerckhove, "Passion and Precision: The Faith of Marshall McLuhan," *Second Nature*, March 31, 2014, https://secondnaturejournal.com/passion-and-precision-the-faith-of-marshall-mcluhan/.
53 Walter J. Ong, SJ, "Communications Media and the State of Theology," *Cross-Currents* 19, no. 4 (Fall 1969): 465.
54 Ong, *Presence*, 13.
55 Marshall McLuhan, "The Reversal of the Overheated Image," *Playboy*, December 1968, 133.
56 Jeff Berner, ed., *Astronauts of Inner-Space* (San Francisco: Stolen Paper Review Editions, 1966).
57 George Gent, "TV: Papal Pilgrimage," *New York Times*, May 14, 1967, 47.
58 Marchand, *McLuhan*, 196.
59 Marchand, 201–2.
60 Richard Schickel, "Marshall McLuhan: Canada's Intellectual Comet," *Harper's*, November 1, 1965, 64.
61 Bill Kuhns, "'It'll Change What I'm Writing, You Know': How I Met Marshall McLuhan," *New Explorations Weblog Studies in Culture & Communication*, July 16, 2020, https://newexplorations.net/how-i-met-marshall-bill-kuhns/.

Chapter 5

1 Hossein Bidgoli, ed., *The Internet Encyclopedia*, vol. 2, *G–O* (Hoboken: John Wiley & Sons, 2004), 117–18.
2 McLuhan, interview by Norden, 72.
3 McLuhan, 74.
4 McLuhan, 158.
5 McLuhan, *Letters*, 297.
6 Jack Smith, "Tremendous Goodby to the 60s' Concepts," *Los Angeles Times*, December 26, 1969, F11.
7 Stearn, *McLuhan*, 277.
8 Jonathan Miller, *Marshall McLuhan* (New York: Viking Press, 1971), 15.
9 MacMinn, "McLuhan," 14.
10 Barbara Rowes, "If the Media Didn't Get Marshall McLuhan's Message in the '60s, Another Is on the Way," *People*, September 20, 1976, https://people.com/archive/if-the-media-didnt-get-marshall-mcluhans-message-in-the-60s-another-is-on-the-way-vol-6-no-12/.
11 Rowes.
12 Marshall McLuhan, "Living at the Speed of Light," *Maclean's*, January 7, 1980, 32.
13 McLuhan, 33.
14 Frank Stroud, letter to Corrine McLuhan, 2, available at https://www.facebook.com/mcluhanestate/posts/fr-stroud-remembers-his-time-with-marshall-mcluhan-during-the-last-two-days-of-h/1425177497591405/.
15 Stroud, 3.
16 Stroud, 1.
17 Marchand, *McLuhan*, 275.
18 Rowes, "If the Media."
19 Marchand, *McLuhan*, 276.
20 Stroud, letter to Corrine McLuhan, 3.
21 David Cronenberg, "The Film Director as Philosopher," interview by Richard Porton, *Cineaste*, September 1999, 6.
22 Paul Levinson, *Digital McLuhan: A Guide to the Information Millennium* (London: Routledge, 1999).
23 "Shoulda Been Dead," *This American Life*, January 17, 1997, https://www.thisamericanlife.org/50/shoulda-been-dead.
24 Kevin Kelly, "How Computer Nerds Describe God," *Christianity Today*, November 1, 2002, https://www.christianitytoday.com/ct/2002/novemberweb-only/11-18-31.0.html.
25 Kelly.
26 Katelyn Beaty, "Geek Theologian," *Christianity Today*, July 15, 2011, https://www.christianitytoday.com/ct/2011/julyweb-only/geektheologian.html.
27 Louis Rosetto, "Why *Wired*?," *Wired*, March/April 1993, https://www.wired.com/story/original-wired-manifesto/.
28 Stewart Brand, "Scream of Consciousness," *Wired*, March/April 1993, https://www.wired.com/1993/01/paglia/.
29 Gary Wolf, "The Wisdom of Saint Marshall, the Holy Fool," *Wired*, February 1996, available at http://yoz.com/wired/2.01/features/saint_marshall.html.
30 Shannon Trosper Schorey, "'What's the Relationship of Technology to God?': A Q&A with Wired Co-founder Kevin Kelly," *Religion Dispatches*, June 16, 2016, https://religiondispatches.org/kevin-kelly-interview/.
31 Kevin Kelly, "Nerd Theology," *Technology in Society* 21 (1999): 391.
32 Kelly, 392.
33 Joshua Meyrowitz, "Morphing McLuhan: Medium Theory for a New Millennium," keynote at the Second Annual Convention of the Media Ecology Association, New York University, June 15–16, 2001, available at https://media-ecology.wildapricot.org/resources/Documents/Proceedings/v2/v2-02-Meyrowitz.pdf.

Conclusion

1 Clare of Assisi, *The Lady: Early Documents*, ed. and trans. Regis J. Armstrong (New York: New City Press, 2006), 146.
2 Assisi, 161.
3 Assisi, 165.
4 Assisi, 172.

5 Ugolino di Monte Santa Maria, *The Little Flowers of St. Francis*, trans. W. Heywood (London: Methuen, 1906), 91.

6 Saint Alphonsus Liguori, "The Spiritual Communion," Vatican News, accessed July 29, 2021, https://www.vaticannews.va/en/prayers/the-spiritual-communion.html.

7 Teresa of Avila, *The Way of Perfection*, ed. A. R. Waller (London: J. M. Dent, 1902), 182.

8 Anthony R. Lusvardi, SJ, "We Should Stop Filming the Liturgy of the Eucharist," *America*, November 25, 2020, https://www.americamagazine.org/faith/2020/11/24/livestream-mass-liturgy-coronavirus-stop.

9 Lusvardi.

10 Marshall McLuhan, convocation address, University of Alberta, November 20, 1971, available at http://projects.chass.utoronto.ca/mcluhan-studies/v1_iss5/1_5art3.htm.

11 "Still Life with Fruit It's Not," Great Past, University of Toronto, accessed July 29, 2021, http://www.greatpast.utoronto.ca/GalleryOfImages/VirtualMuseumArtifacts/PiedPipers.asp.

12 Paul Elie, "The Makings of a Spirituality of Technology: Glenn Gould, Marshall McLuhan and 'Electronic Participation'" (lecture, St. Michael's College, Toronto, October 13, 2016).

13 Antonio Spadaro, *Cybertheology: Thinking Christianity in the Era of the Internet*, trans. Maria Way (New York: Fordham University Press, 2014), 3.

14 Spadaro, 37.

15 Spadaro, 7.

16 Spadaro, 44.

17 Spadaro, 47.

18 Pope Paul VI, *Evangelii Nuntiandi*, December 8, 1975, http://www.vatican.va/content/paul-vi/en/apost_exhortations/documents/hf_p-vi_exh_19751208_evangelii-nuntiandi.html.

19 Pontifical Council for Social Communications, *The Church and the Internet*, February 22, 2002, http://www.vatican.va/roman_curia/pontifical_councils/pccs/documents/rc_pc_pccs_doc_20020228_church-internet_en.html.

20 Pontifical Council for Social Communications.

21 Spadaro, *Cybertheology*, 84.

22 Spadaro, 87.

23 Spadaro, 95–97.

24 Douglas Coupland, "The Extreme Present," Seminars about Long-Term Thinking, November 2016, https://longnow.org/seminars/02016/nov/01/extreme-present/.

25 Marshall McLuhan, *Understanding Me: Lectures and Interviews*, ed. Stephanie McLuhan and David Staines (Toronto: McClelland & Stewart, 2010), 242.

26 Spadaro, *Cybertheology*, 112.

27 Pope Francis, *Christus Vivit*, March 25, 2019, http://www.vatican.va/content/francesco/en/apost_exhortations/documents/papa-francesco_esortazione-ap_20190325_christus-vivit.html.

28 Spadaro, *Cybertheology*, 76.

29 McLuhan, *Letters*, 370.

30 Wallace Stevens, "Of Modern Poetry," 1923, available at https://www.poetryfoundation.org/poems/43435/of-modern-poetry.

31 Wallace Stevens, "Final Soliloquy of the Interior Paramour," 1954, available at https://poets.org/poem/final-soliloquy-interior-paramour.

32 Coupland, *McLuhan*, 81.

Index